CLOSE-UP ON WAR

CLOSE-UP ON WAR

THE STORY OF PIONEERING PHOTOJOURNALIST CATHERINE LEROY IN VIETNAM

MARY CRONK FARRELL

Amulet Books, New York

Caption for previous spread: Catherine Leroy, photographed by French
colleague Gilles Caron, during an operation with the 1st Air Cavalry
Division, Vietnam, December 1967. (© Fondation Gilles Caron)

Cataloging-in-Publication Data has been applied for
and may be obtained from the Library of Congress.

ISBN 978-1-4197-4661-1

Text © 2022 Mary Cronk Farrell
Edited by Howard W. Reeves
Book design by Melissa Jane Barrett

Printed and bound in Thailand
10 9 8 7 6 5 4 3 2 1

Amulet Books® is a registered trademark of Harry N. Abrams, Inc.

ABRAMS The Art of Books
195 Broadway, New York, NY 10007
abramsbooks.com

To the photographers and journalists imprisoned, murdered, or killed while working to get the facts

CONTENTS

viii Map

xii Foreword by Peter Arnett

1 Chapter 1: A Man's War

11 Chapter 2: On the Ground in Vietnam

25 Chapter 3: Worlds Collide in Saigon

35 Chapter 4: Born to the Sound of Bombs

43 Chapter 5: Nowhere Near As Much Fun As You'd Think

55 Chapter 6: They Did Not Accept Me

63 Chapter 7: Itching for Action

75 Chapter 8: Is This Why They Call It Olive Drab?

83 Chapter 9: Proving Myself Under Fire

93 Chapter 10: Not Very Pretty

107 Chapter 11: Like You've Never Felt Alive Before

117 Chapter 12: Jumping for Joy

129 Chapter 13: A Door Opens to the Sky

139 Chapter 14: Everything Rotted

149 Chapter 15: A Big, Professional Success in Every Way

159 Chapter 16: Rumors and Gossip

171 Chapter 17: Battle for Hill 881

181   Chapter 18: Front-Page Pictures

193   Chapter 19: Cồn Tiên, Hill of Angels

201   Chapter 20: Thirty-Five Pieces of Shrapnel

213   Chapter 21: A Bombshell for Tết

221   Chapter 22: The Enemy Has a Face

235   Chapter 23: Return to Huế

247   Chapter 24: Photos "First Class"

259   Chapter 25: The Biggest High of All

266   Epilogue

271   Author's Note

274   How a Camera Worked in the 1960s

278   Glossary

284   Timeline

286   Notes

296   Selected Bibliography

299   Acknowledgments

301   Image Credits

302   Index

CHINA

Điện Biên Phủ

Hà nội

LAOS

NORTH
VIETNAM

GULF
OF
TONKIN

Vientiane

THAILAND

border between
N. & S. Vietnam

Huế

Đà Nẵng

Quảng Ngãi

Bồng Sơn
Kontum

IA DRĂNG
RIVER

Chư
Prong
Massif

Pleiku

Kim
Sơn
Valley

CAMBODIA

Central
Highlands

SOUTH
VIETNAM

Iron
Triangle

Bein Hoa

Saigon

MEKONG RIVER

INDOCHINA
1965–1966

0   150
MILES

Mekong
Delta

SOUTH
CHINA SEA

The Republic of Vietnam*

A government established in the southern city of Saigon** whose leaders often subverted the rule of law and democratic norms, causing problems for the United States. The United States supported the government and sent money and military advisers to organize and train South Vietnamese military forces, called the Army of the Republic of Vietnam (ARVN).

Democratic Republic of Vietnam

A Communist government established by Hồ Chí Minh in the northern city of Hà Nội. In 1954, Ho's followers the Việt Minh formed the People's Army of Vietnam (PAVN), called by Americans the North Vietnamese Army.

National Liberation Front of South Vietnam

A Communist organized armed resistance movement in South Vietnam. It fought against the ARVN and the US military. Its members and guerrilla fighters, the People's Liberation Armed Forces (PLAF), were called the derogatory name "Việt Cộng" by Americans.

---

*   The American spelling of Việt Nam, "Vietnam," is used in this book to reflect American perspective.

**   The American name "Saigon" is used in this book. Today, the city is named Hồ Chí Minh City.

I met Cathy Leroy when I was a young war photographer in Vietnam, and she was already famous for her pictures in *Life* magazine. I was very impressed that she was as brave and as professional as my male photographer colleagues. In later years, Cathy and I became friends in Los Angeles, where she had moved, and I was with the Associated Press bureau there. We both covered the 1992 Los Angeles racial riots, where I saw again how daring and talented Cathy was in such a dangerous crisis. In the years before her death, she would visit the AP bureau and we would lunch at a nearby dim sum restaurant and talk about the old days in Vietnam.

–Huỳnh Công Út, known professionally as Nick Ut, a Vietnamese American photographer for the Associated Press (AP), winner of both the 1973 Pulitzer Prize for Spot News Photography and the 1973 World Press Photo of the Year for "The Terror of War," depicting children in flight from a napalm bombing during the Vietnam War

FOREWORD

Civilian photographers, working with skill and daring along-side American soldiers fighting the Vietnam War, produced images remarkable for their graphic depiction of combat. Among them was Catherine Leroy, a young French woman who was inspired to become a war photographer by photos she had seen published in Paris newspapers and magazines. In her three years in Vietnam, she took photos striking in their immediacy and technical proficiency that were widely published by the Associated Press news agency and in the major photo magazines *Life* and *Look*. But her contributions to the uniquely voluminous Vietnam War photo archives have been largely overlooked in comparison to the pictures taken by male professional photographers from mainstream news organizations, such as Larry Burrows, Eddie Adams, Horst Faas, David Kennerly, and Huỳnh Công "Nick" Út.

In the mid-twentieth-century United States, there were growing numbers of professional woman photographers, generally assigned to cover routine news stories at home. However, news managers sent all-male staffs to Vietnam and earlier wars such as the Korean War. They saw no place in war reporting for women. So, Cathy's being in Vietnam was extraordinary—women simply were not players in photojournalism at the time.

I first met Cathy in the Associated Press news agency's Saigon bureau in early 1966 in the office of our chief photographer, Horst Faas, a Pulitzer Prize winner for his Vietnam pictures. He was assembling a team of freelance photographers to meet the growing demand from newspapers for frontline photographs of the war. Cathy was twenty-one years old, around five feet tall, and slim, with her braided blond hair hanging down to her shoulders. She spoke limited English, but she radiated enthusiasm, and she had an expensive Leica camera that she was just learning to use. Horst Faas was impressed with Cathy's determination and hired her, paying the going rate of fifteen American dollars for each of her pictures used by the Associated Press.

Cathy faced many dangers as she began covering the war. Two Associated Press photographers had been killed in action in 1965, as well as the legendary photojournalist Dickey Chapelle, the first American woman journalist killed in combat. The male Vietnam combat press corps did not welcome Cathy, and she was patronized and ridiculed. And the military made limited concessions for the privacy of the women journalists. Cathy brushed aside the disapproval. She had discovered that politeness opened no doors for her. She mastered an earthy vocabulary of French-accented profanity to use against military bureaucrats who tried to stop her path. She won the admiration of the American infantrymen and marines she accompanied into battle for weeks at a time. In the field, the solders loved her jaunty personality and bravery.

As a correspondent for the Associated Press, I sometimes worked alongside Cathy covering American infantry units in 1966 and 1967. One trip I recall was with her and photographer Michel Renard was a week-long patrol with soldiers of the US First Cavalry Division along the central coast. We slogged through muddy paddy fields and mangrove swamps, watching villages burn to the ground and ducking firefights with the enemy. In the evenings we chewed on canned military rations and crouched over our legs with lighted cigarettes to burn off the leeches, just like the soldiers were doing. Cathy later wrote a note to assuage her mother's concern about personal hygiene in the field, "I just go behind a tree when I need to pee."

Unlike in earlier conflicts, such as World Wars I and II, when the American public was fully mobilized and the press censored, the Kennedy, Johnson, and Nixon governments responsible for the Vietnam War believed that the military and political goals were limited and could be achieved without imposing controls on the press. With free access to combat units, Cathy captured breathtaking images of American soldiers in the heat of battle that were used across newspaper front pages and on magazine covers and featured in television news programs. By her perseverance and bravery, she had become the professional equal of the better-known male photographers who worked for the world's top news organizations.

Cathy deserves to be remembered. She broke through

the barriers of a male-dominated profession and led the way for the bold women photographers who follow her example in crisis areas today.

—**Peter Arnett,** awarded the 1966 Pulitzer Prize in International Reporting for his work in Vietnam during the war

Chapter 1

A MAN'S WAR

Vientiane, Laos

February 1966

Maman [Mom],

A very long and tiring journey. Here
are my first impressions of East Asia.
Vientiane, comparable to a second category
provincial town, but very much dirtier,
many kids (too many), a great many stray
dogs, very poor but welcoming people.

Cath

F-100Ds of the 481st Tactical Fighter Squadron over South Vietnam, February 1966. Early F-100s were unpainted when they arrived in Southeast Asia like the foreground aircraft, but all eventually received camouflage paint like the aircraft in the back. (US Air Force)

Aerial view of Tan Son Nhut Air Base, Saigon, Vietnam, c. 1966. (Eugene McDermott Library, University of Texas at Dallas)

Catherine Leroy* first saw Vietnam from the sky. Jade-green rice paddies spread like chenille over the countryside, miniature villages set in blotches of palm trees, and in the distance, swells and peaks cloaked in verdant jungle. This short flight from the neighboring country, Laos, was the last leg of Catherine's longer journey from her home in Paris, France. It was 1966, and she'd been planning the trip for months.

Now below lay the capital city, Saigon, and the Mekong River flowing into the brilliant China Sea. Her parents and friends did not understand her desire to leave home, travel across the globe, and drop herself into danger. For Catherine, it was simple.

"I want to become a photojournalist, and the biggest story at the moment is the Vietnam War."

Catherine's plane circled over Tân Sơn Nhất Airport while a constant stream of bomb-laden aircraft took off and landed. Fast becoming one of the busiest in the world, the

---

* Catherine Leroy is pronounced: Cat-REEN Li-RAH

airport was a strategic hub for all four branches of the US military engaged in South Vietnam.

Below on an airport runway, a blue-striped Pan American jet crawled by needle-nosed Phantom fighters bristling with deadly missiles. Numerous Skyraiders lined up nearby, prop blades on their noses, bombs under their wings. Esso gasoline tanks, army jeeps, and tiny men scurried like ants between the aircraft.

As the DC-8 pilot waited for an open runway and permission to land, a male journalist told Catherine, "The war is all about men." And he made it clear that he felt women had no business there.

She didn't reply to his pronounced opinion. She'd made up her mind. In fact, nobody had been able to tell her what to do since she was thirteen. As a child, Catherine had been small and slightly built. In response, she developed a strong, rebellious personality.

Catherine had always been fascinated by the pictures in *Paris Match*, France's number one news magazine. So at a young age, she decided to become a war photographer. And though she barely knew how to use a camera and didn't speak much English, at the age of twenty-one, she flew to Vietnam on a one-way ticket.

Stuck in Vientiane, Laos, waiting three weeks for her Vietnamese visa, Catherine started learning to use her camera. Part tourist, part journalist, she traveled about Laos, taking notes and pictures. She visited with Americans who were helping Laotians improve public health, education, and hygiene.

Catherine hoped she might sell a feature story on the aid efforts to the French news agency. But she was impatient to get to Vietnam and cover the real news. To get up close. This was the advice of Robert Capa, possibly the greatest combat photographer in history, and someone Catherine greatly admired. He took what is considered to be the first photograph ever to show the death of a soldier in battle, the "fallen soldier" shot in 1936 in the Spanish Civil War. Capa was the only civilian photographer to accompany soldiers on the D-Day landing at Omaha Beach during World War II. He had been killed by a land mine in Vietnam in 1954, but his words to photojournalists lived on: "If your pictures aren't good enough, you aren't close enough."

Catherine determined to be close enough—close enough to show the world the war. A simmering war that would soon reach a raging boil.

By the 1960s, and for decades to follow in the United States, "Vietnam" was the name of a war, a conflict that ruptured and scarred the American psyche. But Việt Nam is the name of a country in Southeast Asia, and some people there call the conflict "the American War." For them, US military forces were the last in a long line of invaders they resisted and drove out.

Vietnam stretches along the eastern edge of the Indo-chinese Peninsula bounded by the South China Sea. It is about three-fourths the size of the state of California, but in 1960 had twice the population at around thirty-two million people, mostly subsistence farmers living in rural areas.

In ancient times, the fertile land of the northern part of Vietnam today bore tribes that united in strong dynasties until the end of the second century. Then the territory fell under Chinese domination for a thousand years. And yet, the early Vietnamese people rose and wrestled their inde-pendence from China and defended it for the next ten cen-turies. They resisted three separate Mongol invasions, plus one by the Ming dynasty.

Then came France, sending Catholic missionaries in the seventeenth century and soldiers in the 1850s. France claimed lands in 1893 that today comprise Vietnam, Cam-bodia, and Laos. They named "their colony" Indochina. They laid the stones for the bloody conflict where Catherine would begin to make her mark in the world.

One hundred years of French colonialism in Indochina created a small class of wealthy, French-educated Vietnam-ese, but most of the people remained poor, their land taken and turned into large rice and rubber plantations. They labored by the hundreds of thousands for little or no pay, in the fields, in mines, and in homes of the rich.

Indochina developed into the most lucrative colony in the French Empire, enriching companies like Michelin, owned by French brothers Édouard and André. Michelin operated rubber plantations in Vietnam to supply their tire factories, which prospered with the rise of the automobile.

Decades-long Vietnamese resistance grew and flourished during World War II. Freedom fighters attacked French colonials and Japanese invaders, conducting ambushes, sabotage, and firefights. The strongest nationalist leader, Hồ Chí Minh, was inspired by Chinese and Soviet Communism. He modeled his resistance group on Communist theory, a system in which property, goods, and the production of goods are owned in common by the people. Each citizen works and is paid according to their abilities and needs. Hồ Chí Minh's Communist followers became known as the Việt Minh.

During World War II (WWII), the Việt Minh rescued downed American pilots and provided intelligence on Japanese forces. They impressed US leaders with their guerrilla tactics against the Japanese.

Late in the war, when Japanese troops retreated, the Việt Minh seized power and declared independence for the new Democratic Republic of Vietnam, with Hồ Chí Minh as president. The country held its first National Assembly election in 1946 and drafted its first constitution. Once more, the Vietnamese were free from invaders. But the United States' postwar priorities lay in Europe, with rebuilding a strong France, and the French wanted their colonies back.

Vietnam's new freedom proved precarious.

Việt Minh soldiers practice grenade training under the direction of the US Office of Strategic Services (OSS), August 17, 1945. The OSS was an intelligence-gathering agency preceding the modern Central Intelligence Agency. The OSS supplied 200 Việt Minh guerrillas with American weapons and training. (National Archives)

Chapter 2

ON THE GROUND IN VIETNAM

Saigon, Vietnam

26/27 February 1966

Chère Maman [Dear Mommy],

. . . Talking about Saigon now. A very
pleasant town that you would like. People
are insouciant and smiling. Many Americans
in civil dress. All this doesn't give the
impression of being in a country at war . . .

You can write to me at the Continental
[hotel]. I go there every day to pick up
my post.

Love,

Cath

When Catherine arrived in Saigon in early 1966, the National Liberation Front rebels were lengthening dirt tunnels that led east out of the city toward the Cambodian border. Digging by hand, a bit at a time, the Communist rebels expanded a tunnel system begun twenty years earlier in the war against colonial France. Now the guerillas had built an entire underground community to support their resistance to the Republic of South Vietnam.

Concentrated in the town of Củ Chi fourteen miles from Saigon, the tunnels provided guerrilla fighters with living quarters, kitchens, ordnance factories, hospitals, and bomb shelters. The underground network, a secret hideaway, served as both defense and offense against the better-equipped South Vietnamese and US military forces, a stronghold from which to fight.

Rebel soldiers would creep from the ground to craft booby traps for the South Vietnamese and American soldiers.

A rebel soldier crouches in a bunker with an SKS rifle, circa 1968. (US Army)

Preparation of a punji pit, circa 1960. Punji pits were camouflaged holes in the ground filled with sharpened bamboo stakes, typically tipped with poison. (Vietnam News Agency/ Duong Thanh Phong)

They connected trip wires to grenades, released boxes of scorpions or poisonous snakes. A small number of troops could rise from the tunnels to conduct hit-and-run attacks on American marine and army patrols, then ease away into the jungle or disappear underground. The PLAF were supplied and reinforced by the North Vietnamese government, which hoped to reunite North and South Vietnam.

Meanwhile, several hundred miles to the northwest, beginning in January 1966, the US Army First Cavalry Division executed a massive search and destroy mission called Operation Masher. American political and military leaders were not calling US military operations in Vietnam "a war." The mission was to "advise" the South Vietnamese military in its effort to stomp out Communist rebels.

Artillery shells walloped the land from both field guns and warships off the coast. The objective: to clear the region of PLAF rebels. B-52 airplanes dropped bombs sending up geysers of earth. Huge explosions of yellow-orange fire and dense black smoke erupted as aircraft dropped exploding canisters of napalm, a sticky petroleum jelly that can burn hotter than 5,000°F. It is difficult to extinguish even underwater. Napalm sticks to the skin and melts the flesh of humans and animals, causing extraordinary pain, the injuries often fatal.

"Helicopters swarmed over the land," wrote a reporter at

the scene, "buzzing with rockets and machine guns, swooping down into drop zones, disgorging soldiers, kicking out supplies, collecting the wounded and sick, mock assaulting, charging away again, swirling back and forth across the burning land in restless urgent profusion, like furious steel wasps."

Following these air assaults in South Vietnam's central coastal province of Bình Định, from January to March, First Cavalry soldiers went from hamlet to hamlet searching for Communists and their sympathizers, destroying ammunition dumps, fortifications, and stored rice. With cigarette lighters, they set thatched roofs aflame, burning villages in an effort to sweep Communist rebels from the region and discourage their civilian sympathizers. Often soldiers could not distinguish between guerillas and civilians. Many innocent people were killed.

As Operation Masher progressed, throngs of surviving civilians camped along the region's one highway, joining the nearly eight hundred thousand refugees already registered by the South Vietnamese government since the United States had arrived to aid the ARVN.

At the request of President Lyndon B. Johnson, Operation Masher was renamed Operation White Wing to sound innocuous. It was the first of eighteen major US military operations in 1966. American leaders believed the Communist rebels could not withstand these punishing attacks and, in short order, would give up.

Napalm bombs explode on possible guerilla structures south of Saigon in the Republic of Vietnam, 1965. (National Archives)

A PLAF base camp burning in My Tho, Vietnam, 1968. In the foreground is Private First Class Raymond Rumpa of the St. Paul, Minnesota, C Company, 3rd Battalion, 47th Infantry, 9th Infantry Division, with a 45-pound 90-mm recoilless rifle. (US Army Signal Corps)

Catherine Leroy might have had an inkling the Vietnamese would not give up easily. When she was growing up, France had been fighting a war against the Việt Minh. No doubt she had seen pictures of the French Foreign Legion, special forces similar to the US Marine Corps, battling in Vietnam.

"I practically learned how to read by reading the fabulous *Paris Match* of the 1950s. It came every week, and the photography was so tantalizing, such an opening on the world that I realized this was what I wanted to do. Photojournalists were my heroes."

The Việt Minh had declared independence at the end of WWII, but the French were determined to hold on to their colony of Indochina. Hồ Chí Minh traveled to Paris to negotiate freedom for his people, but talks failed. The Việt Minh and the French went to war.

The United States and Great Britain backed the French regime in Saigon, while Communist China and the Soviet Union recognized Hồ Chí Minh's government. These alliances battled through the post-WWII years and into the early 1950s.

The climax arrived in the first months of 1954, when Catherine was nine years old. The Việt Minh attacked the French garrison in the small valley of Điện Biên Phủ. French forces fortified the surrounding hills. Tanks and artillery, barbed wire, and land mines protected French forces.

Hồ Chí Minh in Paris, France, to advocate for independence
for Vietnam, 1946. (National Archives)

But secretly, the Việt Minh constructed a camouflaged road to advance troops, weapons, and antiaircraft guns into the area. They dug more than a hundred miles of trenches snaking toward French outposts guarding the camp.

When the Việt Minh attacked, the French were totally surprised and found themselves completely surrounded and cut off from supplies and reinforcements. The siege continued fifty-seven days and nights, soldiers often fighting hand-to-hand, face-to-face.

Many in France followed news of the battle day by day. *Paris Match* published photos of French Legionnaires battling from their bunkers. The French suffered great losses before they surrendered. The crushing defeat at Điện Biên Phủ ended France's colonial rule in Southeast Asia.

Catherine remembered when the end sounded on the radio, her father wept. Seeing her father's tears made a lasting impression. She may not have understood what this humiliating loss meant for her country, but she felt the depth of it.

Now she was here in Vietnam to see the fighting herself, close up. She carried a letter of introduction from a French press agency, but money and reputation would be made selling pictures to the American press. A chance meeting on the plane had resulted in an important connection for Catherine in Saigon.

A French journalist invited her to stay with him until she found her own place and gave her a contact at an American wire service the Associated Press (AP). News agencies like AP and United Press International (UPI) sent breaking news and photos via teletype along telephone wires to their syndicates of newspapers around the world.

AP's bureau chief, Horst Faas, would be an important contact for a young photographer hoping to succeed in Vietnam.

Chapter 3

WORLDS COLLIDE IN SAIGON

Saigon, Vietnam
26/27 February 1966

Chère Maman,

I've been in Saigon for three days.
I'm taking the time to write to you now
so that you don't worry. Until Monday I'm
the guest in a magnificent house adjoining
Cabot Lodge (US ambassador) and that of
the director of Air France . . . I'll try
and get myself invited somewhere else next
week. Staying at a hotel is too expensive
for my budget.

Love,

Cath

Worlds collided in Saigon, a profusion of color and sound, old colonial infused with new American consumer consumption, wealth and poverty, war machinery and water buffalo. The streets roiled with pedestrians, cars, hand-drawn carts, and pedal-driven taxis called pedicabs. Kiosks selling cigarettes, beef and chicken noodle dishes, or souvenirs lined the sidewalks. A unique mix of Vietnamese, Chinese, French, and American culture flourished. A patter of numerous languages filled the thick air.

In late February, shortly after Catherine arrived, the temperature climbed, on its way toward the height of the hot season in April, with 95°F temps and 95 percent humidity.

"You get used to it," Catherine wrote her mother, "but please send me my pink trousers and the small navy blue top . . . We have to change often here."

Vietnamese women wore the traditional áo dài, a fitted top with snug sleeves to the wrists and long, flowing panels covering loose pants. Local men dressed in loose trousers and shirts. American civilians and uniformed soldiers, marines, airmen, and sailors added to the throng on the tree-lined avenues of Saigon's District 1, a neighborhood of embassies, foreign government and business buildings, and hotels.

If not the weather and people, the architecture was familiar to Catherine. French colonial buildings had been built along the main streets of the city center as if to re-create Paris in this faraway country. Shiny glass windows of a patisserie displayed mouthwatering mille-feuilles and buttery croissants.

Soon after arriving, Catherine applied for press credentials from the American and Vietnamese officials and then went to the AP wire service to introduce herself to Faas. The address was on Tự Do Street, where flocks of reporters and photographers from around the world based themselves. It was a main street running seven blocks from the Saigon River to Notre-Dame Basilica, a copy of its larger namesake in Paris. Walking to the AP office, Catherine would have passed a brisk trade of tailors, jewelers, photography stores, Vietnamese traditional medicine pharmacies, and Chinese tea shops interspersed with bars, cafés, and hotels.

At the Eden building on the fourth floor at the end of the hall, number 422 sounded with the clack-clack-clack of typewriter keys stabbed by the urgent fingers of anxious muttering men, their eyes intense, their cigarettes burned down in their ashtrays. The room buzzed with "frenetic agitation at every minute of the day," she wrote later. "The cor-

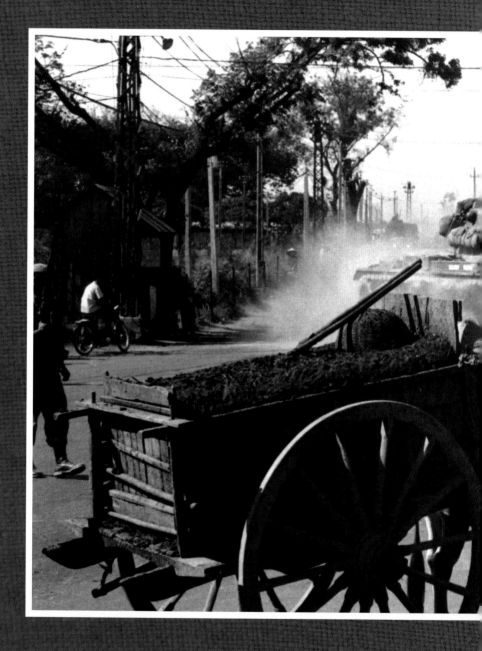

A tank from the 1st Battalion, 69th Armor, 25th Infantry Division, moves through Saigon shortly after disembarking at Saigon Harbor, March 1966. (National Archives)

respondents came and went, always in a hurry. On the floor were helmets, flak jackets, boots, and all the paraphernalia that a photographer would take with him before a hurried departure."

AP had a long tradition of sending out the latest war news. It had been founded by New York City newspapers more than a hundred and fifty years before to get speedier reports from the Mexican–American War. AP's first journalist killed in action died in 1876 at the Battle of the Little Bighorn.

A large map of Vietnam, Cambodia, and Laos hung on the wall of the AP office. Clipped copies of the agency's best stories and scribbled notes covered a bulletin board. Alongside them were pictures of photojournalists and reporters who had been killed covering the conflict, such as Dickey Chapelle, the first American female war photojournalist killed in action. She had died just months before Catherine arrived, struck by shrapnel from an exploding land mine.

Horst Faas, a big man with narrow-set dark eyes and round cheeks, was the head of the AP office. He had been born in Germany during the rise of Adolf Hitler, and was seven years old when the Nazis invaded Poland, launching WWII. Hired at eighteen by an international photo agency, Horst had been chasing war stories ever since.

He'd joined AP in 1956, and in 1962 was assigned as Southeast Asia photographer and AP bureau chief in Saigon. As chief, he gave work to photographers and reporters

Catherine Leroy, 22, in Vietnam, 1967. (AP Images)

and decided which stories and photos would be sent to the New York headquarters for worldwide distribution.

In his four years with AP in Saigon, Horst had seen a stream of young wannabe war photographers come and go. Within two weeks of arriving, they were likely to give up or get killed.

When Catherine walked into the AP office, the men all stopped work and turned to look at her. She pulled herself up to her full height, not quite five feet, took a breath, and asked for Horst Faas.

"She was a timid, skinny, very fragile-looking young girl who certainly didn't look like a—like a press photographer as we were used to arriving for assignment in Vietnam," Horst said later. "She was very young, looked very young. Had a nice pigtail here on the back of her head . . . She came in and introduced herself as a photographer from Paris, and I looked her over like everybody else had in the office . . . and I said, 'My god, here comes another one.'"

"You have experience?" he asked her.

"Yes," she lied.

He reached into his bottom drawer, she remembered later, and plonked three rolls of black-and-white film in front of her. "If you can get anything I can use," he said, "I'll pay you fifteen dollars a picture."

Catherine didn't blame Horst for his initial doubt about her.

"I was a child," she said later, "completely wide-eyed."

She picked up the little canisters of film and asked, "What do I need to photograph?"

He opened another drawer, this one filled with a pile of AP wire photographs.

"I looked at this stack of pictures," Catherine said, "and I knew immediately [the job] I had to do. I got my accreditation, and I went."

Chapter 4

BORN TO THE SOUND OF BOMBS

17 March [1966]

Maman,

Can you buy me a dress . . . very basic,
silk, like my white one—and send it to me
along with my red dress and my navy blue
bikini and the top of the white bikini. I
only have two dresses and I need more. I've
browned nicely and my nose is peeling . . .
I don't think I'll stay six months in
Vietnam, which is a pity . . .

Love,

Cath

Catherine found a room to rent in Saigon and quickly tried to learn the unwritten rules of the press corps based in the city, making contacts with military officials, meeting photographers and correspondents from all over the world, including a couple of young French journalists.

"We make a pleasant team," she wrote her mother. "As I'm obviously a chick [woman], I constantly have to deal with bad jokes, but I think I'll soon do some work with them."

During her first month in Vietnam, Catherine wrote and photographed several feature articles for the French press. For one, she attempted to track down a French mercenary enlisted in the South Vietnamese army but was unable to find him. She attended press briefings from the US military command.

"I've become a great buddy of the head of the American TV channel CBS. He gives me interesting leads. We spent two nights together in a demonstration (it's mayhem in Saigon). The demonstrators are eight to fifteen years old, carrying huge stones and throwing them at the army and the

Americans . . . these kids are beaten up with bayonets. In fact, these kids are really mad, they would kill you without any qualms."

The protesters, mostly Buddhist boys and girls, demanded religious freedom and a new civilian government. They accused the current ARVN military leaders of corruption and selling out to the Americans. The protests continued from late March to early June, but Catherine had come looking for war.

Her mother, Denise, said no one would have imagined Catherine would grow up and head to a war zone. As a child, she'd been frail and plagued by asthma. In the 1940s, the best treatment for respiratory illnesses such as asthma and tuberculosis was fresh, cold air and sunshine. Children were often sent to boardinghouses in the highest mountains in Europe to clear their lungs and gain strength.

Often when Catherine was very young, her mother would put her on the train to Switzerland to spend up to four months in the Alps for her health. Catherine would shed no tears saying good-bye, but later told her mother that "she cried in her heart."

Perhaps her birth during a World War II bombing raid was an omen. Her parents had survived horrors and hardships in France under more than four years of Nazi occupation. Allied Forces liberated Paris on August 25, 1944, and two days later, August 27, Catherine was born during a night of heavy bombing by the Allies.

Her parents, Jean and Denise Leroy, lived in Sannois, a northwestern suburb of Paris. Later the family moved a short distance to the wealthy suburb of Enghien-les-Bains, where Catherine grew up.

Jean Leroy loved classical music and started his daughter learning music when she was six years old. She received private piano lessons from a well-known professor at the esteemed Paris Conservatoire National Supérieur de Musique, founded in 1795.

Catherine had a streak of independence, and as a young teen she gave her parents trouble. "I was always kicked out as a bad element," she said, "and I went to about six schools between the ages of eleven and fifteen. I was always trying to run away."

When she was fifteen, her parents thought a change of course might curtail Catherine's misbehavior, and they sent her to a suburb of London, England, to learn English. But she skipped class and sneaked out at night, taking the train into Central London to hang out in smoky jazz clubs.

"I was a very difficult teenager. I disappeared in England— I was dancing bebo[p] in a jazz club; I wanted to become a blues singer. My mother thought I was completely out of my mind."

When Catherine finally returned home to her English host family, she was packed up and sent back to France. She never went back to school, but got a job in an advertising agency. Though she did well in the job, she soon got "tired of selling wind" and quit. Getting a job at a temporary work company, she put in overtime to support herself so that she could do as she wanted.

At seventeen, what she wanted was to impress her sky-diver boyfriend, so she learned to jump out of a plane. The boyfriend didn't stick, but Catherine joined a formal skydiving club and qualified for her license.

She could have pursued a career as a classical pianist. "I was a gifted piano student, but I never worked as hard as I should have, because it was too easy. To become a blues singer, on the other hand, was a very big challenge."

Somewhere in her teens, Catherine gave up on the singing career and looked for something more adventurous. When a skydiving business didn't work out, she decided to follow those long-ago dreams of shooting pictures like those she admired in *Paris Match*.

During daytime hours, she worked at an employment agency interviewing women who came in looking for jobs. In the evenings, she earned overtime pay monotonously peeling and sticking address labels.

Catherine saved enough to buy a small, top-of-the-line camera made by Leica, a company that continues to make some of the finest cameras in the world today. Next, Catherine saved for an airline ticket. She flew to Vietnam with less than two hundred dollars in her pocket, planning to stay as long as her money held out.

Photojournalism was a tough, competitive, and almost

PARIS MATCH

N° 271 DU 5 AU 12 JUIN 1954 50 Fr.

LA FRANCE
ACCUEILLE
L'HÉROÏNE
DE DIEN-
BIEN-PHU

Sur notre photo : Geneviève de Galard, rapatriée avec les derniers blessés, débarque à Louang-Prabang. Un légionnaire se met au garde-à-vous devant celle qui est devenue son caporal d'honneur sur le champ de bataille.

Cover of news magazine *Paris Match* featuring French Air Force nurse Genevieve De Galard after the siege of Dien Bein Phu and her release from eighteen days as a prisoner of war by the Viet Minh on May 24, 1954. Genevieve inspired the world as the only woman to endure the bloodshed and captivity. Catherine might have seen this photo and been influenced by Genevieve's bravery.

exclusively masculine business. In the United States, Betty Friedan had not yet founded the National Organization for Women, which would ramp up women's fight for equal rights and equal pay. Many Americans still believed in a clear delineation between the roles of men and women. Though it was becoming more acceptable for middle-class women to join the workforce, most held traditional women's jobs such as teachers, secretaries, and nurses. Few joined fields considered men's work.

War and war photography were men's territory. But Catherine refused to recognize these boundaries.

Chapter 5

NOWHERE NEAR AS
MUCH FUN AS YOU'D THINK

17 March [1966]

Maman,

    . . . took a day off to go swimming in
the China Sea . . . It's sweltering hot,
just like a sauna . . .
    I'm starting to make good use of my
Leica, but I need a second camera, one for
black-and-white and one for color . . .
I'll probably decide by the end of the
month. It's becoming an absolute must.
    I hope to hear from you very soon.

    Love,

    Cath

Marines of Battalion Landing Team, 3rd Battalion, 9th Marine Regiment (BLT 3/9), come ashore about four miles northwest of Da Nang Air Base on March 8, 1965. (US Marine Corps)

atherine's first glimpse into international conflict proved interesting but tame, despite the hollers and hoots of thousands of young men with a close-up view of a hot movie star. Ann-Margret was so famous she didn't need a last name. The glamorous Swedish-born American actress, singer, and dancer enthralled US Marines on a tour of Vietnam.

The United Service Organizations (USO) sponsored entertainers like Ann-Margret on tours to visit troops and boost morale. Catherine joined the press corps following Ann-Margret for two days, stopping at different US Marine bases and hospitals and enjoying a meal with the American high command.

On the tour with Ann-Margret, Catherine witnessed no fighting, but found the B-52 bombers quite impressive as they flew out of the Đà Nẵng Airfield to hit targets in North Vietnam. The United States' constant bombing of North Vietnam started a year before Catherine arrived and would continue relentlessly until 1968. Operation Rolling Thunder exploded 864,000 tons of ordnance on

North Vietnam (about the weight of forty-two thousand fully loaded, large school buses, or nearly four thousand Statues of Liberty!).

The first American ground troops had arrived in Vietnam in 1965. Thirty-five hundred US Marines disembarked from their offshore landing crafts, splashing through the surf to Nam Ô Beach. Their mission: to guard the Đà Nẵng Airfield from attack by the rebels.

At the time of Ann-Margaret's visit, twelve thousand marines called Đà Nẵng home base, and bulldozers were moving tons of earth to expand it. America's presence in Vietnam and steady march toward war had started shortly after the French surrendered the colony in 1954. The United States refused to sign the resulting peace treaty at the Geneva Convention, which split Vietnam into two countries separated by a demilitarized zone (DMZ). A DMZ is a strip of land where military weapons, activities, and personnel from both sides are forbidden.

The division of Vietnam was meant to be temporary. The agreement called for nationwide elections within two years to reunify the country and determine the future of an independent Vietnam. US leaders feared the Vietnamese might vote to become Communist, and surrounding nations would follow suit, tumbling one by one like dominoes, threatening democracy around the world.

US leaders used the domino theory to justify secretly intervening in South Vietnam's affairs. When the South

Vietnamese scheduled voting in 1955, the American Central Intelligence Agency (CIA) helped rig elections and bring to power a man named Ngô Đình Diệm. Diệm proclaimed a new Republic of Vietnam and declared himself president in Saigon.

With support from the United States, Diệm refused to hold nationwide elections, provoking rebellion throughout the country. Within months, the United States sent its first direct shipment of military aid and an offer to train the fledgling South Vietnamese army.

The PLAF assassinated government officials, and as Diệm's regime grew more repressive, they stepped up attacks on his army. In March 1959, with support from the Soviet Union, North Vietnam declared all-out military revolution in a quest to unite the country. Many US political and military leaders believed they had no choice but to continue backing South Vietnam. The course was set.

The United States sent four hundred Green Beret "special advisers" to train South Vietnamese soldiers in May 1961, and followed with American helicopter units to transport and direct troops in battle. Soon American "advisers" joined in South Vietnamese combat operations. By the end of 1963, the United States sent more than sixteen thousand military advisers to prop up the South Vietnamese government.

The United States increased military and economic aid that massively escalated the conflict in Vietnam, but didn't

An American military adviser with Vietnamese troops.
(The Vietnam Center and Sam Johnson Vietnam Archive,
Texas Tech University)

declare "war," nor did the administration (the president) seek congressional approval to do so. (According to the US Constitution, only Congress can declare war.)

Catherine arrived in Vietnam just as these US military operations geared up. But it wasn't easy for a young woman to discover what was going on, where it was going on, and how to get herself there.

"As a woman, it's tough to be respected in Saigon," Catherine wrote her mother. "Twenty thousand guys in town, but virtually no European women.

"It's nowhere near as much fun as you'd think . . . I've decided to stay a while yet because I like the work (so to speak). I want to pay my passage home and get back the cost of my operation in Vietnam. All that takes time. But I don't want to go back to Paris penniless and start over . . . that [would] bore me stiff."

Major news outlets like television networks, wire services, the *New York Times*, and *Time* magazine, had their own paid staff in Vietnam. Those photographers earned regular pay for their work. But freelance photographers who came to cover the war on their own like Catherine, also called "stringers," had to pitch their photos and articles to news organizations. They only got paid for the photos selected for publication.

At AP, Horst Faas pored over every strip of negatives developed from the films shot by his stringers in the field. He would hold them up to the light or bend over a light

Horst Faas (right) and AP photographer Malcolm W. Browne
(left) examine film in AP's Saigon Bureau, 1963. (AP Images/
Peter Arnett.)

table, magnifying glass in one hand, hole punch in the other.

"It was the moment of truth," said Catherine later. "Hundreds of times I would come face-to-face with Horst Faas, [hole punch] in hand."

Horst decided which pictures best conveyed what was happening in Vietnam. Those he notched along the bottom, so that in the dark of the developing lab, he could run his finger along the edge of the film and identify which negative to print. A photograph would be printed from the negative and sent by wire to the AP headquarters.

To get the pictures Horst would print, photojournalists faced the same dangers as the soldiers. Horst told them the best shots came in the thick of the action. With pudgy fingers that constantly trembled, he had proven this, working in the field as well as this desk job. He'd been taking pictures in Vietnam since 1962 and won a Pulitzer Prize for his work.

"You can't come [to the scene] half an hour later," Horst said. "The human mechanism is remarkably recuperative. A half hour later the expressions are gone. The faces have changed."

Some weeks after her tour with Ann-Margret, Catherine learned the French press agency had sold two color pages of her photos of Ann-Margret to a Swiss magazine. The agency also bought a few photos she snapped around Saigon.

"I'm not so self-conscious about my technical skills anymore," she wrote her mother. But she offered photos to AP and UPI to no avail.

Catherine's mood improved when she scored her first trip to the field.

Chapter 6

THEY DID NOT ACCEPT ME

8 April 1966

Chère Maman,

Write to me and also send me a box of
Tampax, you never know. Don't forget to put
the money in my account.

Love,

Cath

At press briefings in Saigon, Catherine discovered the Americans sometimes had seats for the press corps on routine military flights between US bases. Each base had an information officer to assist journalists. But often photographers needed to earn the trust of higher-ranking officers to gain permission to go on patrol with soldiers or marines in the field.

Soldiers received orders, and they carried them out. Freelance war photographers didn't get orders from anybody. They decided when and where they might get the best pictures, then tried to find a way to get there.

One day, Catherine managed to gain permission from US Army officials to join a small unit of the 101st Airborne Division on patrol in the Central Highlands of South Vietnam. She hopped a small military plane in Saigon, which made numerous stops heading north. It took her ten hours to reach Kon Tum Province. From there she snagged a helicopter to the airborne command post near Đắk Tô.

The helicopter set down in a small landing zone, where Catherine met Colonel Henry "Gunfighter" Emerson, nicknamed by his soldiers for the six-gun he wore on his hip. As he moved among his officers, possibly talking strategy, Catherine started snapping photos.

The sudden boom of a US artillery gun a hundred yards away startled Catherine. "And I would jump each time it fired a shell, under the amused watch of the officers on whom of course the firing had no effect." No enemy returned fire and Catherine saw no hostile movement.

Fighting in the jungles and rice paddies of Vietnam turned out to be entirely different from earlier wars that the United States had fought, such as World War I and II and the Korean War (1950-53). There was no front line where soldiers met the enemy in battle. The People's Liberation Armed Forces (PLAF) soldiers did not line up rank and file. They hid in the jungles, underground, in the tops of trees, and across borders in the neighboring countries of Laos and Cambodia.

This was called guerrilla warfare. It was their best strategy to fight a larger, stronger, and less-mobile military. Small groups of quick-moving fighters on foot planted land mines and staged ambushes and small hit-and-run attacks.

In the spring of 1966 a few months after Catherine arrived in Vietnam, the United States sent additional American troops into South Vietnam by the tens of thousands. North Vietnam sent Communist soldiers south to support the PLAF. They migrated, ten to fifteen men at a time, through the heavily forested hills and valleys toward the rice paddies and cities of the South.

Colonel Henry Emerson had orders to find and destroy the guerrillas and North Vietnamese soldiers in the Central Highlands. He developed a strategy to try to beat them at their own game.

He mapped the area in a checkerboard, identifying "friendly" and "enemy" squares. His men lay in wait in safe zones along the expected path of North Vietnamese troops and prepared fields of fire. They used grenade launchers and automatic weapons, but the most devastating were Claymore mines. When detonated, they sprayed shrapnel like a volley of machine gun fire.

"Instead of me picking out an ambush for them," Emerson explained, "the decisions were decentralized to the lowest level." In other words, the men in the field took the action they thought best for that particular situation.

His troops camped in the field up to three weeks at a time, on foot, communicating by radio and "moving like ghosts, laying ambushes, and hauling rucksacks with maximum ammunition and minimum rations."

A typical ration was a little canned meat and a few pounds of rice, lasting one man five days until the next supply helicopter. "We went out heavily gunned, carrying ammo, ammo and more ammo, then water," said Brien Richards, a veteran of early Emerson checkerboard missions. "Water and more water, never enough water," said another soldier.

At Emerson's command center, Catherine took photos as the colonel studied a large paper map overlaid with acetate and briefed his officers. He used a pointer stick to indicate a spot on the map highlighted in red, but Catherine didn't understand enough English to follow his directions.

When Emerson asked Catherine if she wanted to ride along on a supply mission, she understood enough English to answer, "Yes!"

Catherine climbed through the wide-open side of the Bell UH-1 Iroquois helicopter. The engine came to life and they lifted off with a rush of air and vibrating metal, the primal whup-whup-whup of the blades filling her ears. The sound of the "Huey" would become as ubiquitous as the chatter of machine guns in Vietnam. The workhorses of the war, Hueys carried soldiers in and out of conflict, delivered supplies, and evacuated the wounded and dead. Near twelve thousand helicopters of all types served over the course of the conflict, with some five thousand destroyed.

Catherine's helicopter flight was short, and soon they plunged into the jungle, lighting on a tiny patch of a landing zone. The men there had gone almost a week without fresh supplies. The company had just survived a severe skirmish in a nearby village.

"The men I discovered were disfigured by tiredness, their eyes vacant. Several of them were lying down, immobile, and mixed with the bodies of some dead [soldiers] that were being slid into body bags with weary gestures."

The helicopter exhaust lifted, exposing a mixture of scents in the humid jungle air—acrid gunpowder, rank sweat,

A Vietnamese guerrilla family, circa 1960. (Vietnam News Service/Duong Thanh Phong)

Injured American troops after battle, 1966.

blood. Catherine went to work with her camera, feeling animosity in the men's stares.

"I didn't look like them, they did not accept me."

In a few moments they'd offloaded boxes of C rations (prepared foods to be eaten on the go), munitions, and mail. They slid the body bags aboard, and Catherine climbed in and crouched next to them. The chopper lifted off, and she headed back to Saigon with her film.

Later, in the AP office, after the film was developed, Horst Faas scrutinized it and notched two of her negatives. Scarcely six weeks into her venture as a photojournalist, Catherine made her first freelance sale to an American wire service!

"In the near future I'll decide whether to stay or go home. I'm leaning toward staying a while longer," she wrote to her mother. But she wanted a telephoto lens for her Leica, and a second camera. "It is unthinkable not to have at least two cameras here. All the other photographers have at least four or five."

Chapter 7

ITCHING FOR ACTION

                                              Saigon
                                    15 July [1966]

     Maman,

     . . . I fit in now (there are still
some gaps in my English, but I understand
perfectly [enough]) to be interested in the
tactical schemes of the American warlords.
I've had the opportunity to meet some
really remarkable people . . .
     These American leaders each go hunting
for Viets in their own way, according
to their respective characters. It is
interesting to compare their different
tactics. The magazine *Newsweek* finds the
idea interesting.

     Love to both,
     Cath

C atherine itched to see a firefight. She'd spent several months in Vietnam without getting any photographs of actual battle. Newspaper reporters might stay at a regiment's or battalion's headquarters waiting for news and details of how an operation played out, but photographers needed to go where the soldiers were fighting to do their work.

They also needed luck. The ambushes and firefights didn't happen on schedule. A photographer had to be in the right place at the right time.

Catherine hired a Vietnamese tailor to make a field uniform to fit her small frame. After her extensive search on the black market failed to produce size five combat boots, she'd come up with size seven and stuffed the toes with newspaper. She carried a backpack with an inflatable mattress, a blanket, a change of socks, and some C rations. It was the rainy season, so she wrapped her ten rolls of film in plastic to keep them dry.

Catherine Leroy, 21, in Saigon, Vietnam, 1966.
(Dotation Catherine Leroy)

Armed with her Leica, plus the new second camera she'd purchased, a Nikon equipped with a small 105mm telephoto lens, Catherine bagged a flight from Saigon to Pleiku Air Base in the Central Highlands. She planned to join the First Cavalry, where, for two weeks, soldiers had engaged in violent clashes with the enemy in the Chư Prông Mountains. The region crawled with North Vietnamese soldiers entering South Vietnam via the Hồ Chí Minh Trail. It was a supply route with an elaborate system of dirt roads, mountain trails, and jungle paths twisting through the mountains for six hundred miles. It ran from the northern capital of Hà Nội through Laos and Cambodia, which neighbored Vietnam on the west. Trails branched off leading into South Vietnam all along the country's western border. Along it, PAVN infiltrated troops and supplies into the South.

The Ia Đrăng, snaking east from Cambodia, cut a sheer valley through the Chư Prông Mountains, providing a natural corridor from the Hồ Chí Minh Trail into South Vietnam's Central Highlands. Catherine learned from the First Cavalry soldiers that six months ago, in November 1965, elements of their cavalry division had pursued North Vietnamese soldiers into the Ia Đrăng Valley and drawn heavy fire.

The fighting raged four days, primarily at two separate landing zones. Americans proved helicopter mobility, artillery fire, and aerial bombing could neutralize the enemy. But they suffered heavy losses, 499 men dead or wounded by the North Vietnamese's agile, close-quarters fighting.

The Battle of Ia Đrăng was the bloodiest American battle in Vietnam to date. And now the First Cavalry was returning to the scene. As Capa had done in the wars he covered, Catherine wanted to get as close to the action as possible.

With a little luck, she would get close to some fighting. She presented herself to the army information officer at Pleiku, getting permission to join the operation. Pleiku was home to an air force rescue and recovery squadron and several army medical units running helicopter ambulances. Due to the difficult terrain, and few passable roads or working railroads in Vietnam, helicopters proved to be the most effective way to bring wounded men in from the field.

Catherine caught an outgoing helicopter on a resupply mission. They flew over double- and triple-canopy rain forest dotted with clearings covered in elephant grass. Then areas of deforestation became visible as they reached the Chư Prông mountains. During the Battle of Ia Đrăng, thousands of North Vietnamese soldiers hid out on the highest peak in the range, Chư Prông Massif. To eliminate their cover, the United States bombed the forest with napalm, the herbicide Agent Blue, and M35 bomblets delivered by B-52 bombers.

Catherine's helicopter landed in a small jungle clearing among hills, dropping her with supplies for B Company of the Second Battalion, Twelfth Cavalry. For a few seconds, she stood still holding her pack, her two cameras slung around her neck. She felt lost, surrounded by men all staring at her.

Army Major Bruce Crandall's UH-1D Iroquois helicopter climbs skyward after discharging a load of infantrymen on a search and destroy mission in Vietnam's Ia Đrăng Valley, November 1965. (US Army)

Then a soldier stepped forward, holding out his hand with a huge smile. "I'm Captain Bird . . . I was told you were coming by radio . . . Welcome . . . Bravo will take care of you." Companies throughout the army and marine corps were identified within their battalions by letter and often referred to by the military phonetic alphabet, Alpha, Bravo, Charlie, Delta, and so on.

Captain Samuel Bird was tall, with his hair cut very short. Catherine learned he was a twenty-seven-year-old career officer who volunteered for Vietnam. He was good-humored, and his men spoke of him with esteem and admiration. He told her a few years ago he'd directed the catafalque guard for President John F. Kennedy's burial at Arlington Cemetery.

Captain Bird had commanded Army Bravo Company in the Central Highlands for four months. His men took the cue and were friendly to Catherine, one volunteering to pump up her air mattress. She made hot chocolate for the men at the command center using the chocolate from her rations.

The next morning, Catherine set out on patrol with the men. They followed single file through the rain and thick vegetation. The soldier out front, some twenty feet ahead, walked "point" to look and listen, to sense danger, and avert any ambush. His eyes scanned the thick jungle for booby traps and venomous snakes.

The second soldier walked "slack" alert for anything the

point man missed. If either soldier saw something that worried him, he dropped flat to the ground. Every soldier following behind did the same. And Catherine, too.

They stayed off the known trails to avoid mines and booby traps, hacking a path with their machetes, or more often their combat knifes, to muffle the sound of their slow progress.

Catherine found the terrain extremely difficult. The monsoon season brought out swarms of mosquitos and turned the earth to mud. "I have to learn to hold on tight, [not] to sink, looking for where to place my foot." She also had to take great care to protect her cameras and her film, all of which could be easily ruined by the drenching rain.

They walked all day, ascending ridges, dropping down rock-walled ravines, wading streams. The red mud caked Catherine's boots. The air, laden with moisture, stunk of jungle rot. The slimy vegetation steamed as it spoiled. The decay, like a ravenous animal, wanted to feast on everything—dank clothing, sweating bodies, any scratch or cut in the skin.

"I'm tired out by the weight of the cameras in my rucksack," wrote Catherine. "I'm tiny. I'm five feet tall and I have no strength." At eighty-five pounds, she kept up with the men while carrying half her body weight in gear.

The company broke for five minutes every half hour, the men collapsing to the ground, leaning against their backpacks. Each soldier carried a rifle and about sixty pounds of gear, including at least two canteens of water, or as many

First Cavalry soldiers on patrol take a rest break during
"Operation Austin" in Quảng Ngãi Province, May 1966.

as eight, canned C rations, ammunition and grenades, plus a poncho. The poncho served as shelter, a stretcher if they were wounded, or a shroud if they were dead.

They hit their target distance by nightfall without meeting any resistance from the PLAF. Catherine had been itching for action. Now her only itch: mosquitos bites.

Chapter 8

IS THIS WHY THEY
CALL IT OLIVE DRAB?

Sunday 4 September [1966]

Chère Maman,

. . . I celebrated my twenty-second
birthday at the Da Nang press office in
the company of lots of marines . . .
I'm getting an iron reputation with the
marines. I'm very proud of it . . . By
the way, if anything happens to me, you'll
be informed within twenty-four hours.
So don't worry if I sometimes leave you
without any news . . .

Love,

Cath

It rained all night. Catherine tried to take cover under the poncho of the radio operator sleeping next to her, but in his sleep, he kept pulling it all to himself. By morning, she was completely soaked.

"Aren't you ashamed?" Captain Bird asked the radioman. "We have a woman with us. A French woman . . . Can't you see how lucky you are?"

All the men burst out laughing.

They grew more comfortable with Catherine after a few days and nights trekking together. Curious, they introduced themselves, asked about her, and made small talk.

Some began to confide. "It's difficult to tell my parents what my life is like here . . ." said one. "I write them all kinds of things to reassure them. The anxiety . . . the loneliness that we face every day . . . I can't tell them about it . . . but today . . . I'm going to tell them about you."

Catherine thought of her parents. They'd be worried about her. Her father would wonder what was going on, his daughter out in the field with a bunch of men day after day. She wrote him.

"At night I sleep in a poncho tent with two or three guys . . . Then comes the big joke— 'When I write to my pals that I slept in a tent with a French woman in a Vietnamese jungle, no one will believe me' . . . In the morning I'm just as dirty and tired as they are, so our relations are very friendly. They forget I'm a girl, I've been adopted."

One day the company stopped near an open space and everyone tuned their ears for the sound of chopper blades, at first faint and faraway, then growing louder, until the pounding *pumpity-pump, pumpity-pump* of the helicopter sounded above them, thrashing everything with a powerful wind as it descended.

All the men gathered in anticipation. It was the first supply drop in four days, but their eyes focused on the big yellow sack thrown from the chopper, the mailbag. The soldiers stood silent and still as a sergeant opened the bag, and each waited to hear his name called. Hands stretched out for the letters, then each man drifted away, sat down, opened the small, sometimes perfumed envelope, and started reading. Some of the soldiers shared the day-to-day events of their wife, fiancée, or family. Others said nothing.

They divvied the food and ammunition from the helicopter between them, hoisted their packs, grabbed their guns, and hit the trail. One day followed the next for several weeks. Catherine filled numerous rolls of film with photographs of the men's day-to-day lives.

They fought mosquitos, heat and rain, and vines that

American 1st Cavalry Division in operation, November 1967.

grew thick and seemed to reach out and tear at their skin, grab onto their olive drab, or coil around their arms or necks. But the enemy did not show up to fight.

Catherine realized this soldiering was drab and boring. She grew exhausted from the hike and carrying the weight of her cameras. The only shower she'd had in weeks fell from the monsoon clouds.

Vietnam was a war without rhythm, a war without a front, no predicting when or if the company would encounter anyone. Catherine decided to return to Saigon and took the next supply chopper back to the base at Pleiku. Then due to stops, delays, and technical problems, spent the entire next day on a small plane to Saigon. She needed a change of luck.

Arriving in the city, Catherine walked down the street in her filthy clothes she'd been wearing in the field for close to a month. They'd been drenched with rain, soaked with sweat, plastered with mud, and mashed with bugs. People turned to stare, but she ignored them as she walked down the sidewalk in the stifling heat. The bluish haze of exhaust from the traffic made it hard to breathe.

She was glad to reach the AP office with its ever-chattering teleprinters. Passing the journalists writing their latest stories, she slumped into a chair and scribbled a few captions for the pictures she'd taken.

Overwhelming weariness filled her to the bone, but Catherine waited for her film to be developed and to see how her pictures turned out. She glanced through them, one of Captain Bird at his command post with a map in his hand, his men gathered near. Others showed a soldier reading a letter, the radioman talking into what looked very much like a phone from home with its tightly curled cord, soldiers at ease, and soldiers hiking up a rocky incline.

It had been two days since Catherine left the company, the trip back a series of hurry up and wait. Now she stared at the faces printed on glossy paper. Surreal, she thought. Did she really meet them? She needed sleep.

Down on the street, traffic was thick with "thousands of rickshaws, jeeps, GMCs, stretch black limos carrying officers of the American high command, a tangle of Japanese high-power motorbikes with their crackling sound ridden by very young Vietnamese."

Catherine beckoned one of the small Renault taxis that came in blue or beige and shortly arrived at her room. It wasn't a home, but it was home for now. She stumbled through the door, tossing her dirty clothing on the floor on the way to the shower.

Once clean, she fell on the bed, aware for only a few minutes of the ceiling fan creaking, "painfully pushing the sticky air" around and around. Her limbs numb with exhaustion, Catherine slept through the night and the next day.

A US soldier reading mail during "Operation Austin," May 1966. In the background stands Dan Rather, the CBS reporter who would later replace Walter Cronkite as the *Evening News* anchorman.

Chapter 9

PROVING MYSELF UNDER FIRE

Saigon

20 September [1966]

Chère Papa,

. . . I've [had] one day to prove
myself: They expect me to break my neck
every hundred meters. There would be ten
guys to help me up, but all would be lost.

I walk around dressed like them (not a
pretty sight), eat like them, twice a day I
tell them I'm fed up of seeing your faces, I
go behind a tree when it's time to pee . . .

Love both of you . . .

Cath

American 1st Cavalry Division in operation, November 1967.

ogether, North and South Vietnam formed the shape of an S. The border between them, the DMZ, cut the top curve from the bottom. Just above the bulge of the bottom curve, fifteen miles inland from the sea, lay a small nest of green river valleys ribbed with rugged foothills. Families tended abundant rice paddies in the fertile region, as they had for generations.

Americans called the Kim Sơn Valley the Crow's Foot. US intelligence suggested it was home base for a battalion of PLAF, possibly a thousand armed guerrilla troops, reinforced by the North Vietnamese.

In September 1966, American B-52 air strikes hammered the jungled hills surrounding the Crow's Foot for two days. Operation Thayer was the largest US air assault in South Vietnam thus far. Following the bombing, a storm of helicopters shuttled roughly two thousand men of the First Cavalry into the highlands surrounding the Crow's Foot. Catherine flew aboard the third helicopter in the first wave of the attack.

"The Huey suddenly loses altitude, the air warms up, becoming burningly hot as we lose altitude. The helicopter's two machinegun operators open fire. It's what they always do. It makes a fantastic noise and the burning-hot machine gun spent cartridges ricochet everywhere inside the helicopter. At our feet, a hundred meters below us, are dried-out paddy fields surrounded by undergrowth."

Seven months ago, in Operation Masher, First Cavalry units swept through the Crow's Foot, clearing out the enemy, destroying the guerrillas' ammunition and supplies, and burning villages. The army resettled villagers, but some came back to their lands and tried to reclaim their lives. Some joined the rebels and North Vietnamese soldiers who had come back after escaping Operation Masher.

Now, the First Cavalry was returning. Units would circle the Crow's Foot, sweep down from the hills and kill or capture large numbers of enemy combatants in the valleys.

Nearing the landing zone, where the first two choppers had spit out their men, Catherine's Huey dropped into range of enemy fire.

"Everything happens . . . with extraordinary violence. The first salvo firing . . . The helicopter zigzags, everyone holds on tight so as not to fall into the void. More torrents of fire . . . one of the two machine gun operators dives forward, his body held in the void by his safety belt; he is covered in blood.

'. . . Everybody down . . .' screams the sergeant. Bullets hail through the open doors and graze over our heads. The other machine gunner, bare-chested under his flak jacket, is still firing. His whole body is vibrating with the machine gun's movements. From time to time, he turns his head toward us. He is covered with sweat."

The chopper descended, hovering over the grass.

"Get out . . . Get out . . ."

Catherine jumped. "[My] horrible stomach cramp disappeared as soon as I touched the ground following the sergeant." Blood pooled on the dirt by her feet. She stepped over the limp body of a soldier, then dropped into the grass like the others, though it was barely high enough to hide them, and certainly would not protect them from bullets. As fast as they could, they scrambled across the ground on their hands and knees to reach cover at the edge of the landing zone.

The shooting intensified, the staccato stutter of automatic weapons coming from all directions. Catherine huddled next to the sergeant, whose bulk made her feel protected.

"Are you OK? Not too scared?'" he asked.

She couldn't speak. Her plight raced through her mind. "I'm out of breath, my legs are weak and my head completely empty. In addition, I'm lying on my cameras. I'm completely dazed by the noise of the M16s all shooting at the same time. Several cartridge cases slap my face. My stomach has gone cramped again."

Pressed to the ground, Catherine pulled herself together and snapped photos in the midst of the deadly chaos. No more helicopters landed in the vicinity. Her group of about twenty men, alone, faced an enemy they could only detect by the bullets flying over them.

Catherine Leroy (background in center, very small and not wearing a helmet) with US 173rd Airborne Brigade patrol, photographed by French colleague Gilles Caron, Thung lũng Shau, Thừa Thiên-Huế Province, December, 1967. (© Fondation Gilles Caron)

"The gunships are coming. We're going to make mince-meat of the Viets," joked the radioman. Two tiny dots in the distant sky drew closer, growing larger until two big-bellied planes loomed above them. One after the other, they dived toward the ground, releasing their rockets before veering up to gain height straightaway.

"The rockets tear through the air, followed by smoke trails, they explode around us. The roar is horrendous, the ground rises up in enormous clouds of dust."

Within half an hour, the enemy retreated. The fighting was over for now. The radioman reported to base. The company took stock: two men lightly wounded, five seriously wounded, three dead. The dead were rolled in their ponchos, the wounded nursed by the medics.

"On the surface I was extremely cool under fire. I didn't show any emotion; in fact, I didn't show anything," Catherine wrote later. "But when I went back to Saigon, sometimes with human brain on my fatigues, the horror of it would hit me, and I would sleep for twenty, thirty hours straight."

Rain started to fall; soft drops splatting on leaves soon grew to a roar. The downpour drenched Catherine's clothes, plastering the fabric to her skin. She grew cold, very cold. It was nearly dark before two medivac helicopters dropped down to pick up the wounded and the dead. A supply chopper landed to give the men clean battledress, socks, and mail in the yellow sack.

"Everybody, food . . ." ordered the captain. Not C rations,

but hot beef steak and potatoes, and vanilla ice cream. The men ate from small paper plates, M16s slung over their shoulders, shivering under their ponchos. Night descended wet and cold, a series of nodding off and waking.

The next morning, the men put on their packs and took up their guns. They only went a short way before stumbling on five enemy soldiers, bodies in shreds. They picked up three AK-47s and moved on. Catherine strode with them, her camera strapped around her neck at the ready.

Fighting in the Crow's Foot and Kon Tum Province would continue, Operation Thayer running into Operation Irving, followed by Operation Thayer II. When Catherine had enough pictures or ran out of film, she rode a supply chopper out.

"I always felt guilty inside….Within forty-eight hours I would be in Saigon, have a long shower and rest. I would be in a French restaurant where the food was nice."

But she never stuck with the easy life, taking two days to sleep, get her clothes laundered, write letters, and then she went back to the field, looking for fighting to photograph.

Chapter 10

NOT VERY PRETTY

20 September 1966

Chère Papa,

   . . . Although work is tough because of
all the male competition (I am in fact the
only woman war photographer), I do very
well out of it. You would be proud of your
daughter if you saw her shaking hands with
[General] Westmoreland and curse in English
just like certain colonels in the Marines
with more decorations than General de
Gaulle himself . . .

   Love to both of you . . .
   Cath

Twenty-four hours after leaving a battle scene, Catherine might find herself in a village like Cổ Lũy, in Quảng Ngãi Province. This hamlet near the DMZ had been PLAF territory for two years. The previous night, a South Vietnamese army battalion surrounded the village. At dawn, they attacked and gained control.

At 10 A.M., the heat was suffocating. The villagers had been rounded up. Three hundred women, children, and elderly men crowded under a tent enclosed with barbed wire. The shade offered little respite from the unrelenting sun.

Catherine arrived with US Marines under the command of Colonel Van Daley Bell Jr. on a mission termed pacification–a policy that was designed to protect civilians and assist in stabilizing the area from the Communists. The first item of business was to register the villagers and question them to discover if they sympathized with the Communists.

A Vietnamese officer sat at a school desk. The line of villagers was long, the stack of paperwork high. A small boy in rags clutched a tiny pack of rice in his hand, mesmerized by the officer, who repeatedly took out his white handkerchief to wipe sweat from his face as he questioned the villagers one by one.

A wrinkled old man trembled, taking his turn with the officer at the desk.

"How old are you?"

"Seventy."

"Do you have any children?"

"Yes, three."

"Where are they?"

"My two eldest sons are in Đà Nẵng. . . The youngest is with a relative in Saigon."

The officer handed the questionnaire to the man, who bowed respectfully several times.

"Đi . . . Đi . . ." said the officer. "Next."

Peasants in the countryside totaled 80 percent of Vietnam's population. The PALF rebels depended on them for food, shelter, intelligence, psychological support, and new recruits. Villagers were vital to the rebel fighters' survival and hope for victory, provoking a tug-of-war between the rebels and the US-backed South Vietnamese. Both sides wanted influence and control over the rural people and their loyalties.

From 1955, the United States had pursued a policy of pacification, trying to aid economic, social, and political reform in rural areas and keep villagers safe from the guerrillas. Pacification aimed to win the hearts and minds of the Vietnamese people. Advocates hoped it would transform

A Vietnamese woman with a baby watches as a US soldier takes a man for questioning, circa 1966–68.

South Vietnam into a modern society, but the escalation of American military involvement in 1965 doomed pacification.

Military and political leaders assured the American public that Vietnamese peasants were being located to safe zones. In reality, US forces increasingly wielded search-and-destroy tactics, clearing out villagers to better isolate the PALF. After burning people's homes, the United States directed bombers and artillery fire to hit the area, then unleashed chemical defoliants to kill the vegetation. US forces labeled these former villages "free-fire zones," meaning anyone spotted was a target.

The US military uprooted hundreds of thousands of people from their ancestral lands and eradicated their livelihoods. Trucked to prepared hamlets, the people gathered their families and tried to begin new lives. Uncounted numbers of civilians perished, innocent bystanders to the conflict. They were commonly shot on sight when US soldiers thought they might be PLAF or sympathizers.

On this day, before entering the village of Cổ Lũy, Americans had air-dropped pamphlets explaining they had come to roust the PALF and transfer peasants to a safer area. Catherine watched as a mother sat on the ground breastfeeding her baby while reading one of the pamphlets she'd been given.

Catherine slipped among the women and children with her camera, a professional detachment on her face, but a great tenderness in her heart.

"Compassion," she said later. "That's the word that comes to me. I think we were all looking to show what the war did to people—on both sides. Yes, we were very subjective. I don't think, in a situation like that, you can be anything but subjective."

Other women and children gathered in a Catholic church partly demolished by the military assault. Marines had a supply of used clothing on a table. In silence, mothers jostled into a line, and each person received a shirt or pants, two pieces of soap, and two chocolate bars.

Marines discovered a network of guerrilla tunnels in the village, and Catherine followed along on Colonel Bell's tour to check them out. At a tunnel opening, the colonel questioned one of his officers.

"Do you think they can stay in there for long?"

"A week ago," one marine offered, "three miles from here the Vietcong killed around ten people in broad daylight and mutilated the village chief."

The colonel kneeled near a tunnel thinking it over, then turned to the marines. "Everyone take a shovel and fill in all these . . ."

The squawk of a loudspeaker announced medical checkups would be "given by their American friends." A tent went up, and a captain and two medics stood ready, cases of medication on the ground.

Catherine stood by to get images and hear the conversation as the first patient approached with timid steps. The

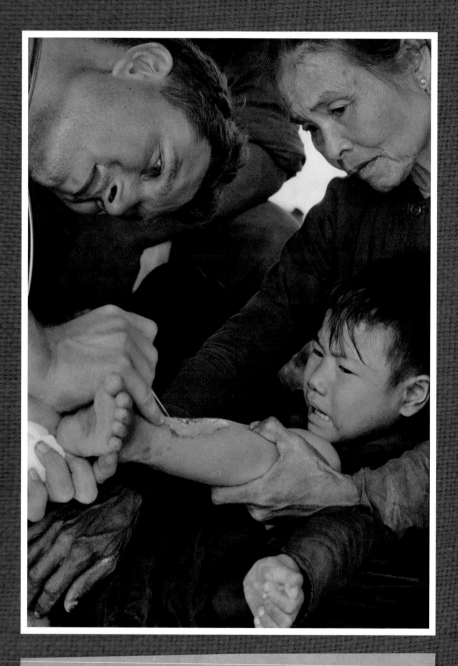

A US Marine Corps doctor treats child, Cổ Lũy, Quảng Ngãi Province, July 1966.

woman carried a small girl in her arms who was crying, the child's leg "clumsily bandaged with a dirty cloth." The woman laid her on the ground and they all squatted around her.

"... Not very pretty ..." the doctor said. He uncovered the wound, cleaned it, applied ointment, and bandaged it with fresh gauze. "I'll see her again tomorrow."

Catherine noticed the marines making lunch for the villagers. One heated and stirred pea soup in a large pot, rivers of perspiration dripping from his face.

A whipping wind and clatter of blades announced a helicopter landing nearby. Catherine recognized the officer who jumped from the chopper, Marine Lieutenant General Victor Krulak. He was responsible for all the US Marines in Vietnam.

Marines were assigned to the five northern provinces of South Vietnam bordered by Laos to the west and the DMZ to the north. Their territory went from rice paddies on the coastal flats to mountains thick with jungle. Most of the South Vietnamese people in the region clustered in villages and smaller hamlets.

General Krulak believed that search-and-destroy missions in the villages caused more problems than they solved. He supported a program where small groups of marines lived among the people, helped with village projects, and provided security from the Communist rebels.

"Anything that moves in the hinterland ought to be fair game—a target. But anything that moves in the highly populated area is a potential friend," Krulak would argue. "Basically, I kept insisting to Westmoreland . . . to anybody else who would listen . . . that first and foremost we had to protect the people . . . The Vietnamese people are the prize. *If the enemy cannot get to the people, he cannot win.*"

Krulak was one of the few people who challenged General William Westmoreland, commander of US forces in Vietnam. "I saw [it] as wasteful of American lives," Krulak said, "[and] promising a protracted, strength-sapping battle with small likelihood of a successful outcome."

Now he jumped from the helicopter and was met by Colonel Bell and the South Vietnamese army officer in charge.

Krulak glanced quickly around him. "When will it be finished?" he asked.

"In two days' time, General," replied Colonel Bell.

"Okay, that's good."

The helicopter churned air noisily, and the general was away as quickly as he had come.

"The soup is ready. There is a general scrum. Women are squashed by children. Everyone holds out an empty bowl or ration box. The toothless smiles of the elderly make a somber picture. 'Two ladles per person,' suggests a marine. The level of soup in the big bowl goes down . . . scraggy arms are still being held out to be given soup." The villagers are told more soup will be served later in the afternoon.

The Vietnamese officer remained at his small desk with his pen and pile of questionnaires. The day had grown hotter and the people waiting in line waved their hats to fan themselves.

Catherine went with a marine unit leaving Cổ Lũy, the villagers' faces on the film in her pocket, faces she hoped would appear on paper continents away. She didn't know what would happen to the faces she left behind. Would the villagers be resettled in a safer place with plenty of food and shelter? Or would they join the hundreds of thousands of refugees scratching for survival in squalid camps? Would the children live to see an end to this war? Catherine and her camera could only bear witness to what showed true on their faces in a single moment in time on this day.

US Marines serve soup to Vietnamese children in Cổ Lũy, Quảng Ngãi, July 1966.

Chapter 11

LIKE YOU'VE NEVER
FELT ALIVE BEFORE

Chère Papa,

    . . . When you see war, you realize
that everyday problems really are banal,
and bourgeois life is no fun. I don't
really feel as if I'm working. Let's say
I'm walking around with my eyes open. My
pockets are light and I'm enjoying this
bohemian life.

    Love and kisses to both of you . . .
    Cath

A marine holds a wounded comrade while under fire near the
Demilitarized Zone, or DMZ, during Operation Prairie in
Vietnam, February–May 1967.

The weeks flew by like days. Catherine photographed marines on Operation Prairie, their fiercest fight since landing in Vietnam. The series of engagements raged for six months at the southern edge of the DMZ, on a backbone of hills the marines had named Mutter's Ridge, Razorback, and Rockpile.

Catherine revealed an innate news sense and relentless purpose, seeking images that would impact people with the power she herself had long felt emanate from news photographs. And she discovered the exhilaration of combat.

"I was so scared sometimes, so scared; I really never thought I was going to get out of this alive," she said. "But when it was all over, and when I was alive and unhurt, like the time when I had a bullet in my canteen, the release of fear gives you a rush, a high of just being alive; you are alive like you've never felt alive before.

"It's not something that's pleasurable in a sensual sense. It's pleasurable in the sense of sheer animal survival. It's your primary brain, your reptilian brain; you are alive as an animal is alive. It's very low and very primal."

Catherine captured these feelings in her photographs of men experiencing all the varied aspects of battle. Her camera was not at a distance, and neither was she. In combat, soldiers forged strong bonds within a matter of minutes. Facing the same enemy bullets, Catherine felt the same connections.

"Friendship, camaraderie, generosity; all of this is what you have in time of war. People reveal themselves without their masks."

If she didn't have compassion for the people she photographed, Catherine saw no sense in picking up a camera.

"Her pictures reflect this affection, for they are rarely heroic," observed *Life* and *New York Times Magazine* photo editor Peter Howe years later. "These are not portraits of a warrior class but of ordinary, frightened, and often bewildered young men trying desperately to stay alive, and relying upon each other to pull off this seemingly impossible feat."

Catherine was one freelance photojournalist among many "who roam untiringly through command posts looking for leads."

"Being there, where the others aren't," Catherine said, "had become a real obsession."

An injured marine receives first aid while under fire near the DMZ during Operation Prairie in Vietnam, February–May, 1967.

"Frequently, I have to confront several staff photographers chasing the same story. Among them is one of the best, the young [Đặng Văn] Phước. Everywhere before anyone else, his hair disheveled, always in a high spirits, with his handful of words of English, and five cameras."

Tim Page, another photographer who came to Vietnam barely out of his teens, and a daredevil wounded in combat several times, noticed Catherine's nerve and initiative. "She's a tiny *mouche* [fly], a mosquito-like person," he said. "She had this dogged perseverance. She was always popping up with a picture."

Catherine caught a rhythm in a war where there was no rhythm. Though she never knew what the next day would bring, the next hour, or sometimes even the next moment, over and over again, she loaded her camera, looked through the lens, advanced the film, snapped the shutter, one, two, three . . . times.

Catherine became attuned to the slightest noise, smallest movement, and briefest gut feeling. Growing acutely aware of her surroundings, she had started to make decisions unconsciously about when to move in for a closer shot, when to stay still, when to shift direction, and when to dive for cover.

In the back of her mind, she knew when her roll of film would run out, when to conserve and wait for the perfect shot, and how to reload without wasting a second. She made snap decisions, her index finger pressing the button and her thumb cranking the film as fast as she could.

Catherine Leroy, photographed by French colleague Gilles Caron, during an operation with the 1st Air Cavalry Division, Vietnam, December 1967. (© Fondation Gilles Caron)

"For a war photo," Catherine said, "you have to be shocked. There has to be a shock that happens and it has to happen in the space of a second, that you feel something, that you are disturbed, that you are stirred. It's something that's done with sensitivity."

In Vietnam, it was not difficult to grab a camera, click the shutter, and take pictures of blood and broken bodies. Catherine wouldn't settle for that. She strived to gain a physical closeness, but more extraordinary was the emotional proximity of her pictures. She focused on the moment when some aspect of war touched someone, soldiers and civilians alike. She captured the collateral damage, the random cruelty inflicted by war.

Chapter 12

JUMPING FOR JOY

Thursday 1 December [1966]

Chère Papa,

. . . I think the next six months will
be very important for me. I've shown my
photos to the boss of _Time_, who advised me,
if I have good stuff, to send it to _Life_.
I think I'm going on an operation with the
First Cavalry, known as First Cav, in the
high plateaux for about a week.

Very warm hugs and kisses . . .
Cath

Catherine's view from a helicopter of a Vietnamese woman and baby on a dike of rice paddy, Mekong Delta, Vietnam, January 1967.

Catherine ranged over all South Vietnam's varied villages and countryside. She walked the Mekong Delta south of Saigon with "rice paddies as far as the eye can see, just a few villages in between, where you are likely to be shot at . . . water up to [my] chest, the camera held above [my] head, the only concern being to keep it dry, under the jeers of the watching soldiers."

Once, climbing out of a rice paddy onto a dike, she was scratched by cactus needles. They ripped through the left knee of her fatigues, which made it easier to pull out the needles poking into her skin. But at the end of the day's march, the knee throbbed painfully.

Catherine traveled north to the DMZ "marching for unending weeks in the sweltering heat, spending nights in a muddy hole, going back to Saigon in overheated airplanes, boredom and tiredness."

She tromped with soldiers through steamy terrain with an eye out for snakes: python, cobra, viper, and krait. The snakes that weren't poisonous were giant constrictors.

"The jungle, the jungle, the jungle. The terrain is impassable, where Viets are walking around ten meters away. In short, it's great fun!!!!" she wrote her mother.

"The marines are really great guys. The young marines in particular are very impressive: calm, very relaxed, these tough youths do a real professional job.

"I went on a night patrol with them. Four days on an operation with a marine colonel: forty-seven, a boxer's features, and colorful language . . . with three wars to his belt, plus extensive war medals . . ."

Catherine trudged with the marines through green blades of elephant grass sharp as razors and growing higher than the tallest man's head. Soldiers called it "wait a minute grass . . . Wait a minute, my hand is cut. Wait a minute, my boot is caught."

The demand for war news came chiefly from Americans, so Catherine chiefly photographed US forces. She enjoyed the feature story she photographed with South Vietnamese paratroopers on a ground operation.

"I had a nice time with the Vietnamese paras. They are great friends. I know everyone in high command and in the division, I visit them when I don't have too much work on my plate."

The ARVN Airborne became one of most highly decorated of all the South Vietnamese army units, its service continuous from 1951 as part of the French-aligned Vietnamese National Army. The paratroopers were all volunteer, as was the entire South Vietnamese army.

An estimated one in nine citizens of South Vietnam would serve in the Army of the Republic of Vietnam at peak enlistment, including regular forces and regional and village-level militias. But as the United States increased troop levels in Vietnam, its initial mission to train and modernize the ARVN seemed to be forgotten. Not until the United States' decision in 1969 to start withdrawing from the war did this effort step up, transforming the ARVN into one of the most highly trained forces in the world.

Less than a year after leaving home with little more than a camera around her neck and no experience taking pictures, Catherine had become a veteran. "In Vietnam, most of the time it was extremely boring. Exhausting and boring. You walked for miles through rice paddies or jungle—walking, crawling, in the most unbearable circumstances. And nothing was happening. And then suddenly all hell would break loose."

She'd made contacts with American military press officers and learned to position herself in the action.

"Always being on the lookout for newsworthy events means that you are much more exposed than the average soldier. When there is a skirmish, the action is there. All the ingredients are there to get to work. But it is not easy. The majority [of photographers] get discouraged."

The South Vietnamese Airborne Division practice a parachute jump, circa 1955. (US Air Force)

Catherine no doubt had her own moments of discouragement. "Work is tough at the moment, but I'm keeping up my spirits," she wrote her parents. "I have visa problems . . . I'm rather worried. This is not the time to be thrown out of the country.

"It's been going on for nine months . . . Yesterday I met the Vietnamese boss of the security ministry. It will be sorted, but it kills me, you have to run around everywhere, wait, explain your good faith."

She admitted, "Got back yesterday without having sold anything. I'm broke. A friend will lend me some money. I think things will go better at the end of the month. I want to have a rest, but have neither the time nor the money for it at the moment."

But after just ten months in Vietnam, Catherine's career began to click. Editors took notice of her photos from Operation Prairie, prompting UPI to run a feature story on her and her work in Vietnam.

She wrote her parents, "I'll send a few photos to [Black Star] agency in New York to show them my work. It's one of the biggest American agencies and it would really help my plan to go and work in the United States one day."

If Catherine were taken on by the Black Star photography agency, she would receive wider distribution and recognition, and most likely earn more money for her photos. Black Star, one of the most well-known and prestigious American photo agencies, promoted their photographers'

work and syndicated and resold it around the world through subagents and to other US publications for reuse. When editorial or commercial jobs came to the agency, they were passed on to Black Star photographers.

It wasn't long before Catherine heard back. She wrote her mother, "A letter from Black Star that I translated found that I am a very good photographer. They want me to send them photos . . . Unfortunately they have two staff photographers here and can't give me any ideas for a story. I have to find them myself."

But she was eager for the challenge. "I want to buy myself a third camera soon, [but] I really need some money. Can you send a check with a banker's receipt? Urgent . . ."

Catherine spent two weeks on an operation with a 101st Airborne Division battalion in Kon Tum Province. Many of the army airborne soldiers, known as the Screaming Eagles, had joined the army specifically because they wanted to jump into combat.

But the Screaming Eagles had not made a single combat jump in Vietnam. Helicopters proved a more efficient way to move men and materials.

One day, Colonel James Lawton Collins Jr. pulled Catherine aside. They had become friends, and he knew she was

The evacuation of a mortally injured marine during Operation Prairie, Hill 484, Quảng Trị Province Hill 484, October 11, 1966.

an experienced skydiver. He told her in confidence that General Westmoreland, a former paratrooper, had approved a jump. The colonel invited her to go with his men on a practice run in early January.

Permission would still need to be granted from the higher-ups, but Catherine was thrilled. This was proof the military officers respected her. They'd noticed her professionalism and grit.

She would be the only member of the press to participate in the first combat jump in Vietnam. She'd have exclusive pictures. A big scoop for a journalist. Maybe her photos would make the pages of *Life*, the large-format, prestigious, and popular American magazine.

"I'm jumping with joy," she wrote her mother. "I'm going to be made an honorary member of the 101st Airborne."

That would come in the new year after Christmas, neither holiday heralded in Vietnam by weather Catherine was used to. Christmas fell in the rainy season, but the rain did not cool the land. The days remained hot, and humidity hovered at 90 percent. Catherine missed this time with her family and friends and the cold nights and snow of her childhood Christmases. On December 25, she went on an operation with the soldiers, to take pictures and to share the anxiety and loneliness.

Chapter 13

A DOOR OPENS TO THE SKY

Saigon

5 January 1967

Maman,

I've been ill for a week, MALARIA . . .
I'm in Saigon, in bed for most of the
time . . . I spent 31 December in
hospital . . . I hope your New Year's
celebrations were much better than that.

Warm kisses . . .
Cath

Catherine started 1967 with a stroke of poor luck, confined two weeks in the hospital with malaria—a disease transmitted by mosquitoes. Time sick meant time without pay. Most of her sales were to AP, and it was clear Horst Faas liked her work, but she still only earned fifteen dollars a photo from the wire service.

Catherine received a letter from *Life*. The magazine had run a few of her photos over the last year and thought they were among the best published by the magazine. Would she permit *Life* to enter them for the year-end awards for news photography in the United States? Yes!

This good news sharpened her resolve to go on the airborne combat jump. She was made for that story! But she did not recover from malaria in time to participate in the paratrooper training mission.

Catherine was far from alone feeling aggravation at the dawn of the new year. President Johnson and his advisers, top military commanders and officers, and men down the ranks to soldiers in the field, all felt frustrated. They should be winning this war, and quick. The American public would begin to lose patience, too.

General W.C. Westmoreland congratulates men of 25th Infantry
Division for their actions during Operation Paul Revere, 1966.
(The Vietnam Center and Sam Johnson Vietnam Archive, Texas
Tech University)

US troop strength in South Vietnam had grown to nearly half a million men in 1967, well surpassing estimated enemy numbers. American forces were armed with superior and far more weapons, from rifles and grenades all the way up to B-52 bombers. They ought to be able to crush the Communist rebels and drive the North Vietnamese back to the north. (Estimates of enemy numbers were later discovered to be inaccurate, deliberately deflated by US military leaders, and lied about to President Johnson and the American public. Even so, the United States was by far a more powerful military force.)

General Westmoreland chose to wage a war of attrition in Vietnam. He believed if he killed enough of the enemy, they would lose heart and give up. But the enemy chose when and where they would fight, and some 70 percent of US engagements with Communist forces were small skirmishes.

Americans killed more men than they lost, but the guerrillas and the People's Army of Vietnam (PAVN) quickly replaced their casualties and came back to fight. US soldiers had a saying, "We own the day, but [the enemy] owns the night."

Westmoreland changed tactics in 1967. He drew up operations to force large numbers of the Communists to come out of the jungles and fight big battles the United States could win. He planned to amass overwhelming American military might and hammer key targets. The first big battle, Operation Junction City, would unfold in an area known as the Iron Triangle. Americans would launch an airborne assault of 845 paratroopers supported by twenty-five thousand ground troops.

Catherine's request to jump went up the chain of command, and the staff at military headquarters in Saigon decided they needed authorization from the US State Department in Washington, DC. They filed the paperwork. And she waited.

The current buzz in the press corps swirled around the disappearance of another young French woman who'd arrived in Vietnam last year. Michèle Ray, a former Chanel fashion model, had come to Vietnam with a hand-held movie camera and a desire for adventure.

Fresh off a publicity stunt where she'd driven a Renault the length of South America, Michèle decided to try it in South Vietnam. She talked the Saigon Renault dealer out of a set of keys and drove north, headed for the DMZ.

Michèle vanished in the Bồng Sơn region in Bình Định province, an area rife with guerrillas.

Catherine thought her reckless and foolish. The woman's empty car was found three days later, some said under a stack of rice, others said covered by palm fronds; whichever, it was booby-trapped with a grenade.

Catherine wrote her mother, "The Viets don't let you shoot film. They start by taking your cameras. If she doesn't die from Malaria or something, her story will not be verifiable and if she manages to shoot a few rolls, they're not likely to be very interesting (Việt Cộng on the march or cooking their rice).

"If she ever gets back, one month or six months, she will use the buzz around her name to sell a film that does not contain much good."

Catherine did not write when the PLAF released Michèle three weeks later, but an earlier pronouncement she'd made regarding the woman remained all too true for photographers in Vietnam: "It is easier to disappear in Vietnam than to win a Pulitzer Prize."

By the third week of January, Catherine felt some anxiety waiting for permission to make the parachute drop. Only civilian and military strategists in the highest echelons knew about the plans for Operation Junction City. Even the men in the 101st did not know when or if they would get the chance to jump.

General Collins had confided to Catherine in December it would happen January 13. But that date had passed and she remained in the dark about the details. She was on speaking terms with General Westmoreland, and knew he'd climbed the ranks from the 101st Airborne. She contemplated paying him a visit, wondering if he would help speed up her paperwork.

Intelligence suggested the PLAF headquarters, which Americans called the Communist Central Office of South Vietnam, was located on one side of the Iron Triangle near the Cambodian border. US military leaders believed large numbers of both PLAF troops and North Vietnamese soldiers camped there, just twelve miles from Saigon, ready to attack.

Smashing the PLAF garrison was one of Operation Junction City's main objectives. Soldiers would parachute into the center of the Iron Triangle to surprise the enemy and search for the headquarters. Ground troops stationed around the Triangle would cut off retreating Communist troops.

Army leaders also believed the mission would be good public relations. Images of paratroopers jumping into combat would remind Americans of victories in World War II. President Johnson hoped that news coverage of Operation Junction City would restore American confidence that victory would soon be achieved in Southeast Asia.

The news Catherine awaited came in late January. She wrote her mother with great excitement. "I've just had the green light from the US State Department for my parachute jump."

Catherine's request and approval opened the door for journalists, men and women, to jump in combat for the remainder of the war, provided they were qualified. Very few people knew that Catherine had earned both first- and second-degree licenses in France.

Since her first time at age seventeen, she'd completed eighty-four jumps, thirty-four of them in free fall, which means she dropped through the air for up to a minute before her chute opened. A friend, Robert Pledge, said Catherine had an "amazing capacity to overcome fear . . . she was terrified the first time and yet jumped."

That first time "was an enormous challenge," Catherine said. "I had to prove to myself I wasn't a coward."

Catherine was thrilled and eager to face that open door in the sky, not for fun, but in combat, and as a journalist. She had no idea when the operation would happen, but she couldn't sit around and wait.

President Lyndon B. Johnson greets American troops in Vietnam, 1966. (US Information Agency)

Chapter 14

EVERYTHING ROTTED

5 November [1966]

Chère Papa,

. . . As for relations with other
people, everything is very superficial,
since I am constantly absent, I haven't had
the time to get to know other members of
the press corps . . .

I find all this very tiresome, I
generally stay at home the two nights I
spend in Saigon between two operations.
That's it.

Write to me.

Love and kisses to both of you.
Cath

To stay in Vietnam, Catherine needed to make money. She pitched several feature stories to Black Star, two that would take her to Singapore for several weeks, and one to photograph shark hunting in Malaysia. The trip would give her a much-needed respite from the violence and exhaustion that characterized her working day in Vietnam.

"You end up going a bit crazy," she admitted to her mother. She would relish "at least one week in a bikini in a sunny village with charming people." Still, she didn't want to be away too long and risk missing a big story.

Though payment for her work remained hit and miss, Catherine stayed hopeful she would eventually build a career.

"It's all a matter of luck, being in the right place at the right time. Now I'm recognized here as a professional. If I still have money problems, I'm not too worried," she wrote her mother. "I'm very young, who hasn't this kind of problems at my age?"

She cut expenses by spending most of her time in the

field, but she still needed to rent a room. Scarce housing in Saigon caused rents to increase, and Catherine moved often, trying to find a decent place she could afford. Sometimes between moves, she bummed a bed from colleagues or acquaintances in the city.

Black Star accepted her proposal for several stories in Malaysia, but she needed money to get there and for food and lodging. She went on patrol with the First Cavalry near Bồng Sơn for six days, hoping to get some pictures that would sell.

Catherine joined Delta Company, Second Battalion, Twelfth Regiment, First Cavalry on its 108th consecutive day in the field. The men had encountered ambushes and booby traps, and in the last thirty days suffered one hundred casualties. She arrived at the command post the day after a serious clash with the rebel soldiers.

A Delta Company lieutenant had been killed. The troops were battered by exhaustion. Morale had plunged. They marched single file along the banks between rice paddies as daylight faded and the sounds of the night prevailed. The men dropped to the ground, giving in to sleep, their packs still on their backs.

The next morning—more of the same. "Orders barked, sections assemble, soldiers resume their walking rhythm. Villages in smoking ruins, paddy fields, heat broken up by torrential downpours, more villages . . . more banks."

Catherine noted an observation Huey. The helicopter

Soldiers from the First Cavalry capture guerilla fighters hiding in a stream in Bồng Sơn, Bình Định Province, February 1967.

flew ahead to inform the captain about the terrain. The radio crackled. The front man sighted two men disappearing into the undergrowth. The observers overhead reported the suspected insurgents had slipped into a nearby pond.

Soldiers fanned out around the pond. Several jumped into the chest-high water and searched the reeds, dredging the pond with bamboo poles. The men hunted for twenty minutes, forty minutes, nearly an hour.

Suddenly a soldier hauled up a young Vietnamese man, pond water sluicing from his skin and clothes. Several men leaped in to help secure the captive, and days of pent-up frustration exploded into fury.

A fist flew, smashing the jaw of the captive as he was dragged from the water. Momentarily unhanded, he dived back into the pond. The soldiers ran after him and pulled him back to shore, then attacked him like a punching bag, beating their captive until he lay still, unconscious.

High on adrenaline, several soldiers fired into the pond, emptying their magazines, hoping to surface the second suspect.

A moment of silence. He popped from the water, smiling, brandishing a Chinese automatic machine gun over his head. But he didn't fire, and like his comrade, was dragged from the water.

No one paid attention to Catherine and her camera.

"A number of soldiers have left their guns and backpacks aside, they want to beat the Vietcong soldier with their bare hands. The captain tries several times to intervene in favor of the prisoner, but no one obeys him."

Sometime later, an intelligence officer and a South Vietnamese interpreter arrived by helicopter. They questioned the prisoners, who gave evasive answers until finally the interpreter hit one in the mouth with the butt of his M16.

Now Catherine was told to stop taking pictures.

She wrote her mother about the photos. "It's extremely rare and is only explained by the physical and moral exhaustion of these guys who had over 100 dead and injured in the last month."

After the war evidence came to light showing incidents like these, and worse, were in fact not rare. "Both we and the Việt Cộng began to make a habit of atrocities," wrote Philip Caputo, a marine who served for sixteen months. "Everything rotted and corroded quickly over there: bodies, boot leather, canvas, metal, morals . . . our humanity rubbed off of us as the protective bluing rubbed off the barrels of our rifles."

But it was not only enemy soldiers who were tortured and killed by Americans. Evidence indicates violence against civilians was pervasive and systematic, sanctioned by US military leadership and perpetuated through military training, policy, strategy, and tactics. Ground troops were trained to call Vietnamese people by derogatory names and racial slurs to reinforce the idea they were subhuman.

General Westmoreland later stated, "Life is plentiful, life

A guerilla soldier captured by US soldiers sits on stream bank, Bồng Sơn, Bình Định Province, February 1967.

is cheap in the Orient." He appointed a war crimes working group to secretly compile thousands of pages of material from investigations of atrocious behavior by American servicemen. Not to punish or deter, but to be prepared if anything leaked to the public. These documents were kept in the dark for more than four decades after the war.

After the guerilla fighter escapes back into the water, he
is recaptured by US soldiers, Bồng Sơn, Bình Định Province,
February 1967.

A suspected guerilla being mistreated by South Vietnamese
soldiers, near Khe Sanh, circa January 1968.

Chapter 15

A BIG, PROFESSIONAL
SUCCESS IN EVERY WAY

Wednesday 29 March 1967

Chère Maman,

. . . I've got the idea into my head
that I've fallen in love with a guy. But
it's a lost cause. He is already married
(he's twenty-four) and furthermore he is
a lieutenant in the 173d Airborne. So I
don't stand any chance at all and I'm very
unhappy . . .

I should have left early this morning
for Cap St-Jacques for a rest and to go
waterskiing, but I didn't wake up and I
missed my plane. I'll use my time this
afternoon to be vaccinated against the
plague.

Warm hugs to you and to Daddy . . .
Cath

Catherine Leroy in combat jump gear, Operation Junction
City, Biên Hòa, Vietnam, February 22, 1967. (AP Images)

Catherine received a summons to US military headquarters on February 22. "Do you still want to [jump]?" she was asked. Yes, she did.

The army arranged her travel to the 173rd Airborne Brigade headquarters at Biên Hoà. She reported the next day. Mission success depended on the element of surprise, so all details remained embargoed. Catherine spent the day with the paratroopers restricted to barracks, awaiting orders and filled with suppressed excitement.

The tension stretched until late afternoon when Army Airborne commander Colonel Robert H. Sigholtz drove up in a jeep. He had a reputation for courage and humility, and his soldiers worshiped him. The whole battalion left the barracks and gathered as the colonel climbed atop his jeep to speak to them.

"Guys, we're going to jump tomorrow," he announced in a loud voice. Cheers erupted.

"We will not jump in North Vietnam," he continued. Disappointed noises sounded from men who wanted to drop into enemy lands and assault the heart of the Communist regime. He told them they would jump into the Iron Triangle near the Cambodian border.

"We'll be the first to jump [in Vietnam]," he said, arousing another wave of enthusiasm.

Now the challenge was to sleep, to be rested for action the next day.

At six the next morning, Catherine joined units of the 173rd Airborne Brigade in a convoy of military vehicles heading to the Biên Hoà Airport. Catherine wore the parachute she'd been issued and a pack attached to her parachute harness carried her Nikon and three borrowed cameras. She'd strung her trusty Leica around her neck to take photos after she leaped out the door of the plane.

The parachute felt heavy, possibly because it plus her camera equipment weighed more than she did. Catherine barely reached five feet in her combat boots and weighed only eighty-five pounds, so "small and thin, she was weighed down so as not to be blown away" from the drop zone.

At the airport, 850 airborne soldiers marched smartly to the long line of C-130 Hercules transport planes. Several planes already held a belly full of howitzers, mortars, and big machine guns too heavy for one man to carry. They would be dropped with parachutes, too.

Seventy paratroopers climbed aboard each of the remaining aircraft, except for one. The seventh C-130 in line carried one woman strapped in among the sixty-nine men.

"The men were all quiet as they spent a good length of time strapped in and helmeted, piled inside . . . The engines fired up and with the altitude the air was quite cool. We flew for nearly an hour before we reached the dropping zone."

The men were finally about to realize the dream of all combat paratroopers. Catherine was poised to realize the dream of most all world-class war photographers.

They reached the Iron Triangle.

". . . Let's go . . . Let's go . . ."

The dispatcher issued the order. Catherine and the men reached up to hook themselves to the static line of cable suspended above their heads. The pilot cut speed, the small indicator on the door lit up green. The static line would open the parachute automatically, allowing the paratrooper to exit in good body position. One by one they stepped forward through the door into thin air.

"I had butterflies in my stomach," Catherine said. "The ejection . . . the shock of the parachute opening, then everything became light. The weather was extraordinarily good, in the sky the parachutes were like hundreds of flowers opening their petals below me, blending into the grass landing zone."

They were floating targets and several shots rang out as they dropped into range. Catherine snapped photos on her way down and landed safely. Within ten minutes, 850 soldiers hit the landing zone and scattered for position. Only

two had been wounded by enemy fire. Operation Junction City was under way.

"I'm very proud of myself because I didn't jump into a tree," Catherine later said with a laugh.

Commander General John Russell Deane Jr. had been the first of the 173rd Airborne Brigade to jump that morning. Later in the day, he met with a flock of journalists who arrived on the scene after the jump.

"Where's Catherine Leroy?" one reporter asked, possibly wondering if she had really parachuted.

"We jumped so near Cambodia, she must be over there now." General Deane replied with a straight face. He joked that the United States might have a diplomatic incident on its hands. American troops were supposed to stay out of the neighboring countries while fighting in Vietnam.

Several days later, General Deane came to the press tent looking for Catherine. He slipped a "jumpmaster wing" from his pocket, the coveted star with a circle around it awarded to airborne troopers who achieved sixty-five jumps, which Catherine had exceeded. He pinned the military badge on Catherine's chest.

"That was your eighty-fifth jump. Wear it," he said.

Operation Junction City continued more than a month.

173rd Airborne Brigade paratroopers photographed by Catherine Leroy during her combat jump, Operation Junction City, Vietnam, February 22, 1967

Cavalry units failed to find the Communist headquarters because it did not exist, at least not as a permanent command post. Like throughout the war, enemy casualties numbered ten to one American dead and wounded. The tactical successes did little to change overall strategic results. The North Vietnamese troops and South Vietnamese rebels stayed mobile, avoiding confrontation with large American units and retreating across the border into Cambodia when necessary for safety.

Catherine, with her slight form rarely still and a surplus of nervous energy, left the paratroopers after three days, hunting action elsewhere, looking for the next big story.

She sold black-and-white photos and a write-up about Operation Junction City to AP. *Life* showed interest in several color photos. Catherine was the story in France. Another photographer had taken pictures of her with her parachute and sent them to *Paris Match*.

Back in Saigon, she wrote to her mother, "I've made over four thousand francs this month, [roughly five thousand in today's US dollars] and have ordered lots of dresses . . ." And to her father:

"I was supposed to be the only member of the press corps (over 400) to jump, but at the last minute 2 other guys [military journalists] jumped too . . .

"I'm very proud . . . it's a big professional success in every way. I now know that I will be able to work in the United Sates one day without too much problem. I just have to carry on the way I'm doing now. At the end of the year I will submit my best photos to the jury for Pulitzer and other major prizes, via AP. Maybe I stand a chance of winning a prize.

"I've always thought I should succeed because I never gave in."

Chapter 16

RUMORS AND GOSSIP

10 March [19]67

Mon Chère Maman,

. . . Today, Friday, I've just had a
telegram from the Times in London. They
want me to write two hundred words on what
I'm doing here . . . it's planned for the
women's page . . . I'm in a bad mood today,
I don't know why. Yes I do, I went on two
four-day operations for nothing. Walking
under a blistering sun, my nose is like
a suckling pig, getting bored to death
because nothing exciting happened, and
missing the good stories.
      That's all I have to say. Warm hugs to
both of you . . .
      Cath

[P.S.] My legs are covered with mosquito
bites. I'm going to look for a beautiful
dress—I'm dining tonight with the big boss
of AP . . .

Catherine Leroy receives a pin from Colonel Bob Sigholtz
(left) commemorating her parachute jump with the 173rd
Airborne Brigade in Operation Junction City, 1967. Leroy,
the only woman to jump with the paratroopers, received a
pin with the battalion's slogan "We Try Harder." (AP Images)

"Don't worry, everything's fine." Catherine wrote her mother. But it wasn't. While Catherine celebrated scoring front-page stories in American newspapers and a four-page exclusive photo spread in *Life* magazine, someone in the press corps started a rumor about her.

The whispers suggested she'd gained permission for her parachute jump by having a relationship with a colonel. The rumors hurt and angered Catherine. She had no recourse to clear her name. She focused on her work and took great pride in her parachute jumper's insignia.

"I wear it on my battle jacket, which makes the other colleagues green with envy."

Some male photographers and journalists may have found it difficult to believe that a woman, especially one as young as Catherine, could achieve such success on her professional merits.

"Many were very, very negative . . . really nasty chauvinistic pigs," according to a friend of Catherine's.

Some men didn't take Catherine seriously at first because of her appearance: a tiny, blond, pigtailed young woman. When they saw her compelling photography, they either gained respect for her abilities or found some excuse to tear her down.

Jealous men in the press corps attributed her great photos to luck. But as journalist Michèle Ray wrote later, "It was not a man, but a woman photographer who held the record for the number of operations undertaken—and by a good length. The youngest of us all, at that—twenty-two years old, and knee-high to a grasshopper."

The majority of journalists, men and women, didn't go into battle, but were happy to stay at press conferences at military headquarters in Saigon or at established command centers.

Catherine had as much luck as the next photographer, but her achievements did not rest on it. She did her time in the field. She reveled in the competitive nature of the news business and was fearless. She believed her work, distilling the war down to one, single face at a time, was important. She accomplished what she did because she stubbornly committed herself to the job.

"I think probably she couldn't think of anything better to do, more interesting—more exciting. And God knows, for a while she was absolutely right," explained American correspondent Jonathan Randal. "I mean, she was there, within months she was, you know, she was one of the best-known photographers in the world. I mean, that must have been very heavy stuff for a very young woman. I know it was."

Catherine may have grown a bit cocky. Not long after her jump with the 173rd Airborne, she came upon a marine unit with parachutes boarding a helicopter.

"Oh, I'd love to go with you," Catherine said. When an officer told her no, she pointed to the airborne wings pinned on her shoulder and insisted she was qualified. The way Catherine explained it, the officer became condescending to her.

"He was extremely arrogant . . . I became disagreeable, and it escalated. It was ridiculous."

Stories spread about what happened, most agreeing that she swore at the officer. Some saying she kicked him, which Catherine firmly denied. Another French photographer in Vietnam at the time, Christian Simonpiétri, said the American military assistant responsible for issuing the press cards in Vietnam revoked her press credentials to punish her for insulting a high officer.

Simonpiétri went to lunch with Catherine in Saigon the weekend after the incident. "Without her press card, no more money, no more food, no more nothing to live. She was ruined, so that was a problem."

He intervened on Catherine's behalf, and she got her press card back several days later.

In truth, some American officers and soldiers disliked Catherine, some believing women should stay safe at home and behave like "ladies." Famed British photographer Don McCullin, who flew in and out of Vietnam many times during the war, noticed Catherine alienated herself.

"She had a tendency to use extremely bad language. You know, F-this and F-that . . . the American male chauvinist marine soldier felt that he was defending the world and he was defending the kind of [world where women were safe at home]. They told me so." And Catherine didn't fit the mold.

Catherine admitted she learned her English from US Marines, and that it tended to be colorful. She seemed to take obstacles in stride. "A few people are doing all they can to make trouble for me in my work and apart from Faas they're all b-s."

Indeed, Horst Faas was one of the few men in the press corps to promote the careers of female journalists in Vietnam. There were but a handful of women reporters in 1967. Catherine rarely crossed paths with them, but all the women faced tremendous prejudice and discrimination.

When American freelancer Jurate Kazickas suffered shrapnel wounds and was sent back to the United States to recover, an American general was heard to say the woman journalist got what she asked for.

Gloria Emerson, who covered the war for the *New York Times*, wanted to write about Catherine. "She was a legend, and I had heard about her." Gloria had seen Catherine in action during Operation Prairie. "One was struck by how tiny she looked. Size is not important . . . It's really remarkable how much combat she saw."

Another Vietnam photographer, American David Burnett said, "[Catherine] was a tough cookie and she knew what she wanted, and she was not in the habit of dealing kindly with fools."

The age-old double standard that judges the qualities of men and women differently, also most likely came into play. As illustrated by the mythic stories from Eve to Pandora to Bluebeard's wife, there's been a cultural notion that women's innate curiosity endangers the established social order. Some men would see a female photojournalist as simply curious, voyeuristic, or as debased due to close exposure to men's bodies and violence. But at the same time, they would judge male photographers as selfless and brave, doing crucial work, showing the realities of war to America's families safe at home.

Catherine paid no attention to critics who insisted women had no place on a battlefield, and she gave no credence to those who wanted to tell a salacious story.

"I never really had any trouble being a woman in Vietnam," she said, "in that I was never propositioned or found myself in a difficult situation sexually. When you spend days and nights in the field, you're just as miserable as the men—and you smell so bad anyway . . . I would help them dig a hole, and we would sleep in it, and there was never any problem, ever. The GIs were like my brothers."

Catherine faced the particular challenge of her small stature when joining soldiers in the field for days or weeks at a time. Marching through tough terrain taxed even the most physically fit men. Catherine loaded herself with heavy

camera equipment to the exclusion of other necessities. The men more often than not shared their C rations with her. "She was, by many accounts, one of the more popular photographers with the troops."

Being petite and female, Catherine also faced dangers in the civilian world of Saigon. One evening she went to a dinner meeting with an American writer who planned a book about the war. She'd brought an envelope filled with prints of about forty of her best photos. The meeting went well; the writer liked her work and said he might offer her a contract to work with him on the book.

The trouble came on Catherine's ride home after dinner in a taxi when the driver tried to steal her purse. She slapped him and was able to get away safely, but later realized she'd forgotten the envelope of photos in the cab.

"Horst Faas tells me he can get some of them back from the archives in New York ([but] there are about 1 million photos a year on Vietnam) . . . so I think I'm really out of luck."

Newspapers and magazines would file and save photographs they published, but with no computer system, there was little practical way to find a specific print. There was no time or space to organize and save prints or negatives at press bureaus in Vietnam.

"I had thought I could use these photos for a book, now I

Catherine Leroy and US soldier take a break during operation, Vietnam, circa 1966. (DCL)

can't even show my work, everything is lost or almost," Catherine wrote her mother. "I'm feeling in a completely catastrophic state. I cried all morning."

When she felt emotionally drained, or simply needed a sense of normalcy, Catherine found shopping offered a diversion. The prices for Asian art objects and souvenirs were inexpensive by Western standards, and she sent several packages to her mother.

"I've bought you a beautiful hand-embroidered tea service. That and the other stuff, you can't complain I don't think about you . . . I've just bought [Dad] a wine-red satin dressing gown that is completely hand-embroidered. A kimono like this would suit him down to the ground."

And Catherine finally ordered a third camera for herself, plus two lenses from Tokyo. She eyed a Japanese hi-fi stereo, radio, and record player. It was the "newest thing," and ran on batteries. "I'm going to buy it," she wrote home. "I get too bored in Saigon."

Chapter 17

BATTLE FOR HILL 881

Saigon

8 March 1967

Chère Maman,

   . . . Everything's calm except in the
North . . . The war with the Marines is the
only real hell still in Vietnam . . .
   Constant skirmishes, shortage of
supplies, you can't evacuate the dead and
wounded who are piling up on the tanks day
after day . . .

   Warm hugs and kisses for both of you . . .
   Cath

In the spring of 1967, Catherine made her three-week trip to Malaysia for the freelance work she'd set up. "I went there for a feature on shark fishing. There were neither sharks nor story, but a marvelous feeling of being on vacation."

Catherine soon reverted back into battle mode. At the AP office in early May, Horst Faas told her the hottest spot would be with the US Marines at Khe Sanh. She rushed to catch a military plane north to Đông Hà, a combat base and airfield just south of the DMZ.

Her trip stalled when she was forced to wait several hours at Đông Hà before there was space on an outgoing helicopter. It was late afternoon before she reached the marine base near the village of Khe Sanh. The remote outpost, fortified with sandbags, sat on a hill named 861, which was its height in meters above sea level.

She found a marine colonel and a few of his men examining a collection of automatic weapons. They'd taken the guns off the North Vietnamese killed the week prior in the fight to secure Hill 861. Several of the Chinese-made guns had telescopic sights. One of the marines said that ex-plained the heavy losses they'd suffered taking the hill.

"All of them were killed with a single bullet," he said.

Right then, a zing whizzed by Catherine's ear. A bullet missed her by inches!

"Good God!" the colonel said. "Take off your headband."

She snatched off the white headband she often wore to keep stray hair from her eyes. The bullet appeared not to fluster the marines. One of them, holding binoculars, turned to smile at her, then squatted to continue his lookout to the neighboring hillside.

Little more than a month ago, the low mountains he viewed had been covered by a sixty-foot jungle canopy, the valleys dense with elephant grass and bamboo thickets. Not now. US forces pummeled the hills they named 861 North and 881 South. F-4 Phantom IIs decimated the jungle cover with tons of bombs, and marines blasted the hillsides with artillery shells.

Located about fifteen miles from the DMZ and close to the Laotian border, the region hosted battalions of North Vietnamese troops. The Communists threaded the forest and dense lowland foliage with routes to walk men, weap-ons, and supplies into the South. North Vietnamese soldiers dug in the dirt and reinforced with logs some 250 bunkers to defend staging areas and supply caches. They holed up and continued working to strengthen their fighting positions.

US Marines manned a combat base on Highway 9, the

Marine forward observers of the 3rd Marine Division trying to
spot North Vietnamese Army mortar position from front lines
at Khe Sanh c. 1967-68. (Sgt. J. S. Ryan/Marine Corps Photo)

major east-west road from Laos. The village of Khe Sanh, a few straw huts on stilts housing about fifty civilians, sat a mile south of the Marine Corp airstrip.

Before Catherine left Saigon, Horst Faas had told her the fighting near Khe Sanh had intensified throughout March and April. The week before, the Second and Third Marine Battalions of the Third Regiment had killed roughly one thousand enemy soldiers. But nearly three hundred marines had also been killed, and seven hundred wounded. This was the highest spike in marine casualties since Americans came to Vietnam. Faas wanted pictures.

Opposite Hill 861, where Catherine stood, Golf Company staked position on a slope, getting ready to assault Hill 881. A handful of marines came to fetch the ammunition they'd need. She went back with them.

"I don't think she was afraid of dying, afraid of what would happen," a friend said of Catherine's ventures into battle. "But she was not made of steel. [She was] afraid but determined . . . she remained there getting the shots."

It had been a long day for Golf Company. They rested on the ground as the captain gave instructions to his lieutenants. Two North Vietnamese platoons lay sheltered in a series of bunkers near the summit. The battle plan directed Golf Company to attack the hill from the east, a second marine company to advance from the south, and a third from the north.

At the word, the men climbed to their feet, zipped their flak jackets, hefted backpacks, and shouldered their M16 rifles. They trudged out single file. This wasn't their first hill, and they knew they'd soon be fighting toe-to-toe with the North Vietnamese army.

Golf Company's Staff Sergeant Ruben Santos said, "There was no way of getting them out [of the bunkers] . . . unless you dragged them out after they were dead."

Catherine followed the marines down a gradual decline for about a hundred yards before the ground started to rise. They faced the hill and hiked up the steep slope of red earth. The underbrush had been destroyed.

US bombs had gutted the land, turning the jungle into a jumble of roots, tortured tree trunks, and splintered branches, everything burnt black. The thick smell of napalm, charred wood, and acrid artillery smoke clogged the air.

The marines crossed a bomb crater. Catherine scrambled down the side, the loose earth giving way beneath her feet. She slogged thirty yards to clamber out the opposite edge.

The column advanced, the men "grappling in hand-to-hand with the hillside." As they climbed toward the summit where the enemy waited, holed up in their dirt-and-log bunkers, daylight started to desert them. The first figures approached the crest of the hill.

A blast and chatter of gunfire exploded the quiet. A handful of marines fell dead. In a barrage of automatic rifle fire, their buddies assaulted the ridge a second time. And a third.

"Climbing past the bodies, the leathernecks keep charging. I try to run up the hill which is very steep and muddy. There's no vegetation to hold or pull yourself up with because of the heavy napalm and bombings," Catherine later explained.

"A marine falls not far from me. Voices call for help, screams over the infernal noise of automatic gunfire."

Catherine hugged the ground, aiming her lens between half-burnt sticks, her trigger finger snapping. Soon the falling dusk would render her camera useless.

In the din and rising smoke, a medical corpsman crawled to the nearby fallen soldier. Removing his helmet, he bent over him and tried to stanch the blood.

The corpsman remembered later, "I heard a bang, and I lifted my head out of the trench and saw my friend—it all happened like in some dream—his body started falling . . . there was chaos going on around me but there was absolutely no sound."

When he reached his friend, "The only noise I heard was his heartbeat disappearing little by little. The bullet was in his chest . . . He had gotten shot through both lungs. I found the one entry wound and then I found the exit wound, so I knew he didn't have a chance."

Catherine saw it through her lens, a tableau come and gone in seconds. The corpsman cradled the soldier, put an ear to his chest, heard the heartbeat fade, then raised his face to the sky, looking lost in the bleak landscape.

Members of the 2nd Battalion, 26th Marine Regiment, near Cồn
Tiên, DMZ, May 1967.

The corpsman grabbed the dead man's M16. Swearing at the top of his lungs, he charged the North Vietnamese bunker, firing until the chamber was empty. Then he dropped the gun and ran to give medical aid to another wounded marine.

Catherine cranked her camera and pressed the button again, but had reached the end of the roll of film. The light was poor, anyway. She didn't bother reloading her cameras, but hunkered down as the last light faded. By the time the marines routed the North Vietnamese and captured Hill 881, darkness reigned.

Golf Company staked a perimeter and dug in for the night, the men decompressing, some more stoic than others. Catherine saw one man suffer an attack of hysterics, then sit down next to a dead body and sob.

A squall blew up with heavy rains and 40 mph winds. Catherine found a place to sleep. She wouldn't be able to leave Khe Sanh until there was room in one of the helicopters transporting the bodies.

Chapter 18

FRONT-PAGE PICTURES

Saigon

13 May 1967

Chère Papa,

. . . In short, I'm getting telegrams
from people who I didn't know existed
for years, while at the same time I'm
hated more than ever by known and unknown
enemies. American civilians as well as
servicemen in Saigon. Let's not put the
worst light on it . . . I have some good
friends, those I got to know at the start.

Warm hug and to Mommy, too . . .
Cath

When Catherine managed to get a ride, the chopper was headed to Đà Nẵng. From there she sent her film on the first flight to Saigon. With it she sent a note to Horst Faas, warning him she'd been working with low light. He'd need to develop the film with special processing to raise the negatives' sensitivity to light. She might never see how the photos turned out. Only the best got printed, fewer got sold and published.

When the negatives came across Horst Faas's desk, they caught his attention. "Blasted jungle with only tree stumps standing. A lot of dirt stirred up. Soldiers in between mud and dust . . . storming uphill . . .

"When I saw [them] on my picture desk," Faas continued, "I thought that, in all these years . . . in five years I hadn't seen a single sequence of pictures like that . . . these were pictures that were new." Horst didn't notch the negatives. He sent the whole strip of photos to AP headquarters in New York.

A suspected North Vietnamese soldier with a marine after the siege of the marine base in Khe Sanh, February 1968.

By May of 1967, the close-up faces of war, unique every time Catherine looked through her lens, had become tiny specks in an enormous quagmire. America had sent half a million young men to wage war in South Vietnam. The number killed in action that spring had nearly doubled.

Some five hundred journalists followed American operations that often seemed to repeat themselves day after day. The tropical weather changed, only to get wetter in the rainy season. Catherine never lost sight of what she wanted, but living and working with the soldiers in the field was a constant slog.

When she had arrived, Catherine's sympathies had lain with the American objectives to aid a democratic government in South Vietnam, to squash the Communist insurrectionists, and to prevent the encroachment of the Communist North Vietnamese.

"She went thinking it was a just war, but fairly quickly shifted her thinking . . . realized it was not the war she expected, that many of these kids did not volunteer to be there."

From 1964 to 1973, the US military drafted 2.2 million men to serve in Vietnam. At the time, every eighteen-year-old male had to register for the draft. He was put on a list from which the US government drew names to call men to military duty.

People in America were changing their minds, too. In 1965, when the United States started escalating the war, more than 60 percent of the public supported sending troops to Vietnam. Only small groups of peace activists and college students rallied in protest of the war. Now, two years later, anti-war demonstrations in the United States were growing in size and frequency.

In 1966, one of the most popular songs in America was "The Ballad of the Green Berets." The rousing, patriotic tune was written and sung by a US soldier who'd been wounded in Vietnam's Central Highlands.

But in the spring of 1967, news photographs and film regularly showed American troops torching Vietnamese homes and dropping napalm on vegetation, soldiers, and villages. Students staged demonstrations targeting Dow Chemical, the company that supplied the military with ingredients for napalm.

Protests on college campuses gained momentum. A small but growing number of citizens began to believe America had made a mistake getting involved in Vietnam. Some started to see the situation not as a Cold War power struggle between the United States and the Soviet Union, nor a civil war between North and South Vietnam, but a fight by the Vietnamese for national liberation and independence.

Disillusionment with the war increased as the financial costs rose, biting into domestic programs. That only added to the pain of the rising numbers of American men wounded and

A large crowd at a National Mobilization to End the War in Vietnam direct action demonstration, Washington, DC, October 21, 1967. (Library of Congress)

killed. Men who didn't want to go to war publicly burned their draft cards.

Demonstrators tried to stop troop trains, and religious leaders dumped blood on draft records. Racism became a focus when reports showed Black men were drafted, assigned to combat units, and killed at higher rates than whites.

In 1967, the peace movement went from fringe to nudging mainstream America. The largest protest, in October, drew one hundred thousand protestors at the Lincoln Memorial in Washington, DC. About half of them broke away from the organized event and illegally marched on the Pentagon. This demonstrated a growing willingness by people to break the law, to commit nonviolent civil disobedience in an effort to end the war.

In May 1967, Catherine returned from the fighting near Khe Sanh and for the first time saw the pictures she'd taken on that hellish hillside. She had a moment of clarity.

"The pictures I took of [the] Navy corpsman leaning over his dead buddy on 881 summed up for me my fifteen months of war—I understood then what I was in Vietnam for."

Catherine had come to Vietnam expecting to photograph brave men in battle. In the field among the soldiers and marines, what most touched her was their humanity and compassion. She had captured such a moment in one

(Above) US Navy Medical Corpsman Vernon Wike examines a wounded comrade while under fire from North Vietnamese guns on Hill 881 at Khe Sanh near the border of Laos in South Vietnam, May 2, 1967.

(Right, top) US Navy Medical Corpsman Vernon Wike hears his friend's heartbeat fade, Hill 881, Khe Sanh, May 1967.

(Right, bottom) US Navy Medical Corpsman Vernon Wike at the death of his friend and fellow marine, Hill 881, Khe Sanh, May 1967.

human face, one single black-and-white image. AP wired the photo to news desks around the world. *Life* magazine published six pages of images Catherine had snapped on Hill 881. NBC News showed the pictures.

They had a profound impact on the American public. Across the country, mothers became convinced the corpsman in the photo was their son and phoned AP trying to confirm it. Catherine returned to Golf Company to discover the name of the man she'd photographed.

The corpsman was Vernon Wike, age twenty, nicknamed "the Gorilla" by his friends because of his abundant body hair. When he took a shy look at the photos Catherine took of him, he said, "But where were you? I didn't see you."

Catherine had taken three rolls of film; not all of the pictures made the newspapers, but she was able to hand out prints to the men who recognized themselves.

"I am very happy to find these marines again. We establish a bond of friendship. The sergeant who led me back to the helicopter shook my hand at great length. 'You'll always be welcome,' he said. 'Come back and see us soon.'

"Chère Maman," Catherine wrote, "I'm very happy. After all these long months, this time I was lucky. I was on my own on this mountain, all the other journalists were stuck in [the village of] Khe Sanh . . .

"[I am the] first photographer to have her photos [credited with her name] on the front page of the *New York Times* (since Horst Faas in 1965).

"*Time* said my photos are a reminder of the ghosts of Iwo Jima, I'm almost certain of winning a major prize at the end of the year, the Robert Capa [Gold Medal Award named after the famous combat photographer]. I've made a name for myself now and I have a good chance of getting what I want."

A friend, American correspondent Jonathan Randal, advised Catherine her luck might run out in Vietnam, and perhaps it was time to go home:

"I mean, who was I to tell anybody anything, but I mean I did see the chances she was taking and the danger she was running . . . you know, when people are very, very young, war reporters they think they'll live forever. They don't—they have no sense of—they quite often have no real sense of danger. That's why they do such terrific work."

Catherine had no plans to quit.

Chapter 19

CÒN TIÊN, HILL OF ANGELS

Tuesday 16 May [1967]

Chère Papa,

. . . I'm leaving tomorrow for the
north. There was a violent mortar attack in
Huê this morning. Côn Tiên is isolated and
can only get supplies by parachute drops.
The situation seems to be evolving to a
massive offensive by the Viets.

Warm hugs to both of you . . .
Cath

Catherine arrived in Đông Hà, the operational command center for the Second Battalion, Twenty-Sixth Marine Regiment, late in the afternoon on the second day of Operation Hickory. The news was grim. A line of stretchers rested on wooden trestles, and the medical staff readied supplies and equipment. A medivac chopper churned the air and dropped to the ground.

The battalion had come under a barrage of mortar fire. Twenty men, including the colonel and three other officers, had been hit by shrapnel. Stretcher bearers raced to the chopper to carry the injured to the first aid post.

The vicious attack had come in the region of Cồn Tiên, or Hill of Angels. Each patient wore a label pinned to his shirt or around his neck, identifying him and the nature of his wounds. Catherine was struck by how calm several were, bloodied and bandaged, chatting and smoking cigarettes. Others writhed in silent pain. Doctors hustled to bend over the patients and examine them.

"A young marine, his battle attire in shreds, bites his handkerchief so as not to scream. His two hastily bandaged legs are little more than pieces of bloody flesh . . . He is carried into the first aid post in priority, where he is first of all given an injection of morphine. A doctor examines him and renews his bandages. His jaws are still biting tensely onto his handkerchief, the young marine is staring at the doctor."

"It will be okay, lad . . . don't worry." The doctor reassured him, before turning to his next patient and muttering to a corpsman. "Poor kid. He's going to be amputated . . ."

A helicopter crew readied to head back to the battle site, transporting replacements for the wounded officers, including a new colonel. Catherine rushed to climb aboard.

Côn Tiên rose from the countryside, a barren, bulldozed plateau barricaded by barbed wire in the withering heat and choking red dust. Artillery embankments, sandbagged bunkers, and defensive trenches completed the fortifications built by American marines.

Across the DMZ, a North Vietnamese flag waved from a tall pole. From time to time, puffs of white smoke appeared and mortars rumbled, harbinger of a warning shout.

"Incoming . . . Incoming . . ." Everyone had maybe twenty seconds to jump into a bunker or huddle in a trench before the shells exploded nearby. Charlie, Côn Tiên's mascot dog, would sense the rocket fire and beat the men into a bunker.

When night fell, rockets streaked the sky with light, as the marines answered the shots with shells of their own. Sleep was impossible. Catherine lay on the edge of a hole in the

US Marines treat one of their wounded near Cồn Tiên, DMZ, May 19, 1967.

ground. At each warning bellow, she rolled in. As often as not, someone dove in on top of her.

With the morning light, Catherine scouted for Golf Company, the men she'd met on Hill 881. She found them but didn't dare cross the two hundred yards of open ground to reach them. The marines insisted she ride a tank heading across, promising she would boost Golf Company morale. She climbed on, tucked down among the cases of rations and ammunition, and made the journey safely.

The fight ratcheted up with the morning sun as the battalion fought its way north from Côn Tiên into the DMZ. Marines ran and dived behind any possible bits of shelter. Others hugged the ground, shells bursting on all sides. Golf Company was pinned down, unable to advance. The dust kicked up, covered everything, tasted of ash, and coated Catherine's lips and teeth. She remained with the company taking photos. For several hours, all the men could do was hope to survive the next barrage of rockets and mortar shells. When men got hit, the corpsmen ran to aid them.

Throughout the day, Golf Company tried to break through the enemy line, but failed. Failed again. The marines faced a solid shield of enemy fire. They had not yet killed a single soldier, but thirty marines had been wounded and ten killed. Catherine hunkered down with the men for the night.

In the darkness, US airstrikes hit the PAVN positions in front of the marines, softening the enemy. At 5 A.M., US artillery fire pounded the bunkers and trenches of the North Vietnamese. At 7 A.M., the marines advanced with no opposition, the land rolling out ahead of them, the undergrowth so thick at times the tanks with their steel tracks made slow, lumbering progress.

Catherine crunched forward with the men, who seemed deaf to the incoming mortar fire.

"We were being mortared again and again, and there was nowhere to hide." Catherine tracked a marine in her viewfinder. He advanced with head down, shoulders hunched, hands tense on his M16 rifle. Light and sound exploded—in a fraction of a second several men dropped.

"At first there is a strange sound . . . the sound of a gong, then I fall to my knees. The three cameras I'm carrying on my chest are covered in blood and I try to clean them. I put my hand on my cheek, but instead of a cheek there is only blood."

Catherine sank to the ground, conscious, but unable to call out or get up. Hidden in the grass, she felt terrified nobody would find her. Blood soaked her shirt and pants. Finally she heard a voice.

"I think she's dead, Sarge."

Catherine feared those words would be the last she'd ever hear.

Members of 2nd Battalion, 3rd Marines, fight near Khe Sanh, Hill 881, Vietnam, May 2, 1967.

Chapter 20

THIRTY-FIVE PIECES OF SHRAPNEL

19 February [1967]

Chère Maman,

. . . I don't have any insurance of
any kind, but trust in my lucky stars. I
should already have died 100 times, so you
know I'm not frightened by this kind of
thing. I have become more of a believer,
a young GI gave me a [medallion of the
Virgin]. I'm ploughing ahead . . . His
thing should work. Moreover, I've always
had the impression I will die simply in
my bed, without knowing anything what's
happening, so I'm keeping calm.

Very warm kisses . . .
Cath

Someone shouted for a corpsman, who ran up and knelt in the grass by Catherine. He checked her pulse and pulled out his scissors, snipping expertly through her battle shirt. Her bra suffered the same fate despite her protests.

"Now, now . . . this is hardly the time to be modest," the corpsman told her.

A mortar shell had exploded near Catherine. The explosion ruptured the metal shell casing into small pieces, hurling them in many directions at high speed. These fragments, shrapnel, had ripped into Catherine's body, wounding her head and neck, her back, and both arms and legs. Her jaw was broken, and blood seeped into her air passages, impeding her breathing.

Automatic rifles continued to fire, artillery blasted away. It was too risky to land a medivac. The marines wrapped Catherine in a poncho and laid her on a tank with others seriously wounded. The road back to Cồn Tiên was long.

Several marines walking behind the tank smiled at Catherine and gave her a thumbs-up. When she closed her eyes, she heard them swear.

"She won't make it . . ."

She made it as far as Cồn Tiên, where she was laid on the ground in a line of bleeding marines. The guy next to her had taken it in the belly. "We share a cigarette, then we hold each other's hands very tightly and keep on holding them."

Catherine became conscious of men lifting her onto the floor of a chopper, which transported her to Đông Hà, the marine base she'd arrived at . . . two days ago? Marine Major General Bruno A. Hochmuth walked among the wounded at the first aid post and spoke to the men. His presence and few words gave comfort. When he saw Catherine, he ordered her immediate evacuation to the nearest hospital.

Catherine wanted to open her cameras and remove her film and send it to Saigon. Dried blood caked the latches, and shrapnel had damaged the two Nikons around her neck. Working with desperate fingers, she finally got them open, and handed off the film to the marine information officer who promised to get it to AP.

Catherine inspected the damaged Nikons further and realized she owed them her life. Hanging against her chest, they had stopped the shrapnel from tearing into her vital organs. Clinging tightly to her cameras, Catherine lost consciousness.

She didn't know how much time had passed when she regained awareness and found herself in the receiving area on a hospital ship. The USS *Sanctuary* stood anchored off the coast near the DMZ. She lay on a stretcher among many others awaiting triage—where the wounded were organized

Members of 2nd Battalion, 26th Marine Regiment, transporting wounded soldiers just before Leroy was wounded, near Côn Tiện in the DMZ, May 19, 1967.

in sequence of urgency. When her turn came, the medic was surprised when he lifted the blanket to inspect the label around her neck.

"My God! A woman . . . a blonde," he said. But he went right to work examining her injuries and relayed Catherine to surgery.

After three hours in the operating room, she woke on an iron bunk bed. A rubber tube attached to her arm ran to a bottle of plasma hanging above her. Doctors had retrieved as much shrapnel as possible, but some pieces would stay in her body. Her wounds were stitched and her broken jaw reattached. The staff situated her in a room by herself on the officers' floor.

Catherine barely left her bed for three days and three nights. John Susko, a corpsman she had known in the field, seemed always to be there when she opened her eyes. He had nearly recovered from wounds he suffered a month ago and would soon go back on duty. She figured he had volunteered to help the overworked nurses.

A mirror on the wall drew Catherine to keep looking at the wound on her cheek and assess how much it would scar.

"It's nothing. You're still my pretty French woman," John Susko told her, making her blush.

General Hochmuth also came to check in on Catherine, as well as the commander in chief of US Marine forces in Vietnam, General Lewis Walt. She heard over the ship's loud-speaker that General Walt had come aboard but did not expect him to knock on her door.

He came in, visited a few minutes, and then, a bit awkwardly, pulled a manicure kit from a pocket of his military fatigues. "I can't give you a Purple Heart," he said, "I thought you might find some use for this."

His kindness touched Catherine, as did the care and concern of all the doctors and nurses. The *Sanctuary* neared capacity, and one last helicopter landed on deck with its cargo of wounded men. After filling its six hundred beds, the hospital ship lifted anchor, sailing from the coast of the DMZ roughly a hundred miles south to Đà Nẵng.

An orderly delivered a large packet of letters to Catherine when they reached Đà Nẵng. She didn't know newspapers had reported her wounds and was surprised to see letters and cards from strangers all over the United States offering get-well wishes. A letter from the sergeant of Golf Company caused a swell of emotion to rise in her, as did another from the mother of the corpsman she'd photographed on Hill 881.

Nurses allowed Catherine to get up and walk after recuperating a week. She ate with the officers, about twenty men in blue pajamas. Three times a day, she sat with them at a long table. Between meals, the men spread a sheet of green hospital gauze on the surface, turning it into a game table, a never-ending series of shuffling, dealing, and the slap of worn cards.

Some of the soldiers on the *Sanctuary* recovered and returned to their units. For them, this was an air-conditioned respite from the physical and mental vexations of the field, and the clawing fear and mortal danger. As Catherine

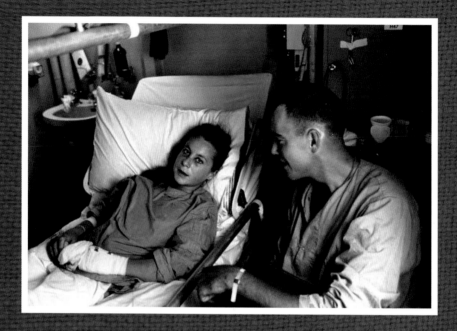

Catherine Leroy, 23, talks with Lt. Robert Brown on May 28,
1967, of New York's Staten Island from a hospital bed aboard
the USS *Sanctuary* in the South China Sea off the Vietnamese
coast. Both were wounded by same North Vietnamese mortar
blast on May 19. Leroy was photographing US Marines moving
toward the DMZ at the time. Brown was the first man to reach
Catherine, and despite his own arm wound, gave her first aid
and brought her out of the battlefield. She suffered multiple
shrapnel wounds and a fractured jaw. (AP Images)

gained energy, her stay in the hospital healed her morale and nerves as much as her body. But that wasn't true for everyone, and the cards dealt were often cruel.

Catherine noticed the young marine she'd seen biting his handkerchief ten days ago at the Đông Hà first aid post. His legs missing, in a wheelchair pushed by a nurse, he trundled the deck for hours, "vacant and wearing a poor smile, everybody falls silent when he approaches . . . But there are also plenty of others . . . with only one arm, one eye, blind, who every evening grope their way, supported by a buddy, to the screening of a film on the upper deck, and who have the scenes described to them, the heroine's silences and the color of her eyes. For all except these unfortunates, the atmosphere on board is euphoric."

The *Sanctuary* left the South China Sea, on course for the American base at Subic Bay in the Philippines, where Catherine recovered for another four weeks. She wrote her parents, calling the thirty-five pieces of shrapnel ripping into her body an "accident."

"The scar on my cheek is almost invisible . . . the neck is passable. The arms are pretty, as for the thighs, they're much better. I can still wear my dresses."

Catherine remained buoyed by the fact she was in the running for a major photography prize. Her hope and excitement spilled over in letter after letter to her parents.

"I want to come back to Europe with money and a prize from the American press (if no one does anything better

Chère Maman,

I'll send you a series of photos I shot recently in Saigon, with close ups, etc. . . . to show you that I'm still very pretty in spite of all. Just a scrape on my cheek and my neck. One day I will take advantage to have my nose done at the same time. And you too, you could have your skin stretched in places where you think it's necessary. We could get a discount for having it done together. And it would be nice to be able to argue with each other again.

before the end of the year) I should be the first woman to get the Robert Capa prize."

Her breezy tone made light of her injuries, and she did not confide how the sounds of mortar fire and close-hitting bombs over the last months had twice burst her eardrums.

Catherine's mother wrote to suggest that when she recovered enough to pick up her cameras, she turn her focus to less dangerous subjects.

The USS *Sanctuary*, a hospital ship. (US Navy)

Chapter 21

A BOMBSHELL FOR TÉT

Tuesday 15 August 1967

Chère Maman,

I wrote to you more than ten days ago and
still haven't had a reply, have you gone on
holiday?

I just got back to Saigon after eight
days . . . in North Đắk Tô (in the middle of
the rainy season, where you die of cold). I
visited General Deane and his paratroopers.
All the people I know have gone, there were
only new faces there; I had a sore throat
and to cap it all I had my period . . .

I got home last night tired and disgust-
ingly dirty. I'll spare you the details, but
the jungle is full of leeches and my bum was
eaten by them for two days, it was awful . . .

I hope to hear from you soon . . .

Everything's fine here . . .

Warm hugs to you both,
Cath

atherine did accept less dangerous photo assignments, but she didn't record the details or write her
parents about them. After about three months, they
lost their appeal.

In October of 1967, she headed back to "her marines"
at Cồn Tiên.

When she arrived, rockets were raining at a ferocious rate.

"Inside the command post bunker the marines huddle
up a few seconds, dust off their shoulders from the dirt that
the violent impacts have made fall from the bags above their
heads, then continue going about their business.

"Another enemy is now infiltrating. By the thousands,
we're being invaded by rats. As big as hideous cats, with
red eyes and snot dripping from their noses. They're everywhere, even managing to squeeze in through the mosquito
nets to bite the marines."

The rats scurried about, as if immune to the earsplitting,
earthshaking explosions.

Wounded men filled the first aid bunker waiting for the
medivac choppers. But the helicopters triggered enemy

fire. Only the best pilots managed to land on this red rock jutting over the DMZ.

If Catherine felt sickened by the killing she witnessed, the horrors of combat, she didn't speak or write of it. She didn't write about it to her mother and father. She didn't record it in her notes. Like the soldiers she photographed, she found somewhere inside herself to hide it away. She erected some insulating veneer that allowed her to continue to function, to continue to look through the lens of her camera and snap the shutter as she followed one unit after another maiming and being maimed, killing and being killed.

Catherine volunteered to risk enemy fire and felt a kinship with the soldiers she stood with. But unlike the men whose tours lasted one year in Vietnam, Catherine could leave at any time.

In the fall of 1967, she withdrew the money she had saved from the sale of her photographs and flew to New York City. Armed with her portfolio, she hoped to advance her career. She knew she stood in the ranks of the best staff photographers in Vietnam, and that it was time to leave freelancing behind.

She was right. Catherine wrote her parents the good news. "My stay in New York was a success. Black Star (the largest agency in the United States, working with all the leading

A radioman confers during 101st Airborne near Chu Lai, Quảng
Province, August 1967.

magazines) is giving me a flat rate of five thousand francs a month plus 75 percent on all the stories sold. The terms are quite exceptional, some people are green with envy."

The end of 1967 was marred for Catherine when General Hochmuth, who had visited her several times when she was wounded, died in a helicopter crash. Then Horst Faas, who had escaped his desk job at the AP office to shoot in the field, was seriously wounded by a grenade. Shrapnel sliced into his crotch and thigh, severing the main artery in his left leg. Horst narrowly missed having his leg amputated and would return to the photo desk on crutches.

In January, however, she received good news. Catherine was notified her work had won a major award! The US National Press Photographers Association gave prizes in numerous categories such as fashion, sports, magazine features, and portraits. Catherine won first prize in the news report category.

The honor was especially sweet, because the second place award went to French photographer Henri Huet. The previous year, Huet's photographs of the Vietnam War had won the Robert Capa Gold Medal. The Robert Capa winner this year would be announced soon.

In Saigon, no good news came from Khe Sanh. Catherine couldn't forget the costly fight for Hill 881 she'd photographed the previous May in that region. The US Marines faced a bigger and more brutal fight at Khe Sanh now. The North Vietnamese completely surrounded the marines in the small sunken valley. Any reinforcements or resupplies had to be helicoptered in, but the enemy had attacked during monsoon season, and low clouds as well as enemy fire made flights difficult.

No one in the American command knew that the PAVN assault on Khe Sanh was a diversionary tactic. Communist leaders meticulously planned a surprise offensive they would spring during Têt Nguyên Đán, Vietnamese Lunar New Year, the most popular holiday for the majority in Vietnam.

Catherine was taking a vacation at South China Sea Beach near the Đà Nẵng Marine Corps base when the attack hit. In the early morning hours of January 30, mortar rounds hit the Đà Nẵng airstrip, and enemy troops attacked the base. An informal ceasefire had been called for Têt so that local troops on both sides could join their families for several days of celebration. It was not immediately clear that the attack at Đà Nẵng was part of a major attack throughout South Vietnam.

US forces put down the attack at Đà Nẵng fairly quickly, but the next morning, Catherine heard fighting raged in Huế, the second-largest city in South Vietnam. Huế was located on the major supply route, Highway 1, midway between Đà Nẵng and the DMZ

"I had brought my bikini and my cameras. I had everything. As fate had it, I never got to use the bikini."

She arranged to catch a helicopter to the Marine Corps support base at Phú Bài and hoped to catch a convoy the rest of the way to the American compound at Huế.

Chapter 22

THE ENEMY HAS A FACE

5 July [1967]

Chère Papa,

. . . Sparks are flying around there . . .
Vietnamese artillery, rockets, mortar
bombs, and so on . . . the marines are
taking awful losses. That's war . . .
I'll keep you posted.
Warm hugs to both of you!
Cath

Over the next twenty-four hours, the scope of the Tết Offensive, as Americans came to call it, became clear. The attack shocked American leaders from the battlefield to the White House. They'd seriously underestimated the number of enemy forces. Some eighty-four thousand PLAF and North Vietnamese troops assaulted military bases and hundreds of cities throughout the South, including Saigon. In the capital, a small unit of elite North Vietnamese Special Forces breached the gates of the US Embassy and battled for six hours before they were overcome by military police guarding the complex.

The Communists believed their concerted attacks throughout the country would inspire a general uprising of the people that would overthrow the South Vietnamese government. As the United States and South Vietnamese fought to regain control of Saigon, the cities of Huế, Đà Lạt, Kon Tum, and Quảng Trị fell to the Communists.

Reaching the American base at Phú Bài, Catherine teamed up with French journalist François Mazure and took off on foot for Huế. The distance was about ten miles, a few hours hike. The city held great symbolism for the Vietnamese, as the former capital of the Nguyễn dynasty, and the city was the hub of Vietnamese culture and intellectual life. Catherine guessed it would be a big battle, and she didn't want to miss it.

Marine Charlie McMahon, escort for a truck convoy, saw Catherine and François walking along the road and offered them a ride north.

"I've been told there's a few snipers in Huế," he said

"It's much worse," Catherine said. "The North Vietnamese hold the city, and you guys are going into a buzz saw."

"I haven't been told this," Charlie said. "I think that's being a little bit exaggerated. They wouldn't send just one squad like this with this truck convoy."

None of them realized how bad it would be.

The Marine Corps convoy cut off about four miles south of Huế, and Catherine and François struck out on their own. Assuming hostile territory ahead, they changed into civilian clothes. To make better time, they rented bicycles from a French-speaking Vietnamese they met along the road. Nearing Huế, they heard the popping sound of bullets as they proceeded down empty streets.

"We were growing nervous and whenever we did see people peering from their houses, François called *bonjour, bonjour,* very loud and friendly, to show that we were French and not American."

Eventually, they arrived at a marketplace in the newer

Civilian refugees in the Congregation of the Most Holy
Redeemer Cathedral, Tết Offensive, Huế, February 1968.

part of the city. A mile north, the old city was circled by a moat and enclosed in a fortress known as the citadel. The fortress walls protected the imperial palace of Vietnam's last royal family, the Nguyễn dynasty.

Catherine and François received no welcome. The few local people they saw avoided them. The racket of gunfire continued, sometimes near, sometimes in the distance. It appeared the Communists controlled much, if not all, of the city. South Vietnamese bombers flew overhead, targeting the thick stone walls of the citadel.

Later in the afternoon, a citizen pointed the two journalists to the Congregation of the Most Holy Redeemer Cathedral for refuge. They found the church and its grounds swarming with some four thousand civilians: old men, women, and children who'd fled there for safety during the previous day and night of fighting.

"The people did not look happy to see us. Hundreds of children surrounded us. They were silent and wide-eyed and hostile, and they pressed against us, pushing in from all sides."

"There were about ten wounded, and one woman had just given birth to a baby. She lay on the floor in front of a confessional . . . the sound of all the people talking and the children crying was incredible, a rolling, continuous roar."

A priest allowed them to stay the night in his room, but the next morning he told them they had to leave. The refugees feared if North Vietnamese soldiers came, they wouldn't be able to convince them Catherine and François were French, not American. Their presence could spark a deadly attack on these people if they were thought to be harboring the enemy.

One boy volunteered to escort them through the neighborhood controlled by North Vietnamese into territory held by American soldiers. They emptied their packs, leaving all their military clothes, even boots, behind.

Catherine hid her American and Vietnamese military identity cards and several cans of exposed film in her bra. "I am only five feet tall and weigh [eighty-five] pounds, and I kept asking François, [who was] an old friend, 'Look at my bosom. Does it look strange?'"

What if it did? Their lives were at risk. They pinned big paper signs on the front of their shirts with the Vietnamese words "Pháp báo chí Ba Lê," translated as "French press from Paris." The priest wrote a letter in Vietnamese confirming they were French journalists. They fashioned a white flag and followed the boy.

They'd gone only a short distance when they ran into a group of North Vietnamese soldiers, dressed in khaki uniforms and carrying AK-47 automatic rifles. The boy frantically waved the white flag, and Catherine and François shouted.

"Pháp báo chí Ba Lê! Pháp báo chí Ba Lê!"

Three of the soldiers confronted them.

"Their faces were hostile, but they seemed calm. I was less afraid now than before. At least the three men were

North Vietnamese soldiers with Chinese AK-47 automatic rifles guard a captured stronghold in battle for Huế, Tết Offensive, February 1968.

real—you could see them, smell them. They were somehow less frightening than the enemy with no face, the only one I had known before."

The soldiers took Catherine's and François's cameras away and tied their hands behind their backs with parachute cord, their manner more thorough than brutal. "I had seen many North Vietnamese prisoners, but they were always in great fear and great pain. This was the first time, suddenly, that their humanity was in front of me."

François offered the letter written for them by the priest, but the soldiers ignored it. They led Catherine and François into a garden surrounding a grand villa, where more than a dozen soldiers had dug foxholes under the trees.

Some of the soldiers came to look, but no one threatened them. Catherine dived for the dirt when an American spotter plane flew over and a South Vietnamese bomber circled. The North Vietnamese might decide to kill them, or American troops might happen by and they could be caught in a clash of rifle fire.

The minutes ticked by, and Catherine tried not to show fear, but she was shocked and shaking. Nearly an hour passed before anything happened. Then the soldiers hustled her and François into a small cottage behind the villa and left them with an elderly Frenchman. The man explained that he and his Vietnamese wife and two daughters were being held prisoner in their home.

As they sat talking, a PAVN officer near Catherine's own

age entered the room. When he understood they were French journalists, he ordered their hands untied and their cameras returned.

Always thinking of the story, Catherine asked if she could take some pictures.

"We said that we had come from Paris to do the story of the victorious North Vietnamese Army taking Huế, and that we were in a hurry to go back to Paris to file our report."

The officer led them back outside. "He seemed very pleased with himself, and as a matter of fact he acted just like some of the information officers I've met in the American units."

The soldiers seemed to relish having their pictures taken, striking what Catherine called "phony heroic poses."

"I thought it was absolutely extraordinary because so far, no one has ever managed to take pictures of a North Vietnamese unit fighting in South Vietnam. This has not yet been seen in the news."

One pretended to throw a grenade, another showed off an American M79 grenade launcher. She photographed several PAVN on a captured American tank. "I doubt that they knew how to drive it, but they all grinned at us like soldiers of a victorious army."

Catherine saw they were well armed with plenty of ammunition, and though she acted as if snapping photos of the enemy was routine, "I was so scared that I wasn't trying to be the brilliant photojournalist." She knew she and François had to get out of there. Sounds of firefights in the city grew near, and she feared they could be in the middle of the battle.

François made the first move, with a painstaking, off-handed remark. "Well, we have to get back to Paris with our story," he said, "so we'll be running along now."

The officer did not object, and Catherine shook hands all around. She said a friendly good-bye as if it were an everyday occasion to visit the enemy encampment. They walked out the gate with their young Vietnamese guide, free, but facing a perilous walk back through enemy lines.

"François," Catherine said and said again, "I'll kiss the first two Americans I meet!"

They found relative safety holed up with a unit of South Vietnamese soldiers and two seriously wounded American troops, whom Catherine promptly kissed. She then tried to get them some morphine from the South Vietnamese. François borrowed their radio to send coordinates to US forces in hopes they could evacuate the bleeding men. Catherine and François bunkered down through a fierce exchange of fire before venturing out again to reach safer ground controlled by US forces.

The next morning, Catherine parted with Francois to join a marine sweep headed back in the direction from which she had just escaped. The marines engaged PAVN and guerrilla soldiers at close quarters, both sides hiding in homes and buildings. Civilians, too, crept and ran from building to building for refuge as they sought to escape the battle. At the cathedral where Catherine had taken safety two nights before, a US anti-tank vehicle took aim and opened fire, its six recoilless rifles shooting in rapid succession.

Screaming, Catherine ran up to grab the platoon leader and shake him. "There are four thousand refugees in there," she yelled. "They aren't VC, they are just people!" The soldiers, towering over Catherine in their flak jackets, grinned at her and stopped shooting.

While the battle for Huế ground on, the Communist attack, or Tết Offensive, collapsed throughout the South. Rushed and overly optimistic, it failed to rouse a revolution and demanded a huge cost. By US estimates, Communist casualties numbered forty to fifty thousand men. The United States did not lose many men in the initial days of the Tết Offensive, but the series of attacks throughout South Vietnam shocked the American public. People had been led to believe US forces were winning in Vietnam and that the war would soon end.

Catherine returned to Saigon with her film from Huế, confident she had a big story. She'd write up the details of her capture and release by the PAVN. She'd have close-up photographs of enemy soldiers. It would be a huge scoop.

Chapter 23

RETURN TO HUẾ

9 September [1968]

. . . The American lieutenant in charge
of information for the Vietnamese paras (a
charming young man) told me one evening
that his bosses suspect me of working for
the French intelligence services . . .
Would you believe it . . . the whole of
Saigon is in spy-fever. Everyone thinks
that everyone else works for the CIA and
even I've been accused of it (absurd!).
Nevertheless, I've just found out that a
French friend was himself one and that came
as a crazy shock. You can't really trust
anybody. I know I'm being watched from both
sides, the Viets and the Americans. At the
moment, I'm a bag of nerves . . .

Cath

The Tết attack on Saigon had not been completely put down when Catherine came from Huế. The capital city ran on a 7 P.M. curfew. The PLAF had entrenched themselves in Chợ Lớn, a heavily populated neighborhood. The US and South Vietnamese military evacuated residents from their homes, then pursued the rebels with bombs and artillery fire. Intermittent violence seethed for more than a week.

The situation depressed Catherine, and the news from Huế was no better. Saigon and Huế had been major targets in the Tết Offensive and demonstrated a change for the guerilla forces. Instead of the rural ambushes where they had an advantage, they attacked targets in the capital and fought street-to-street in Huế.

The battle in Huế grew fiercer as the days went by. It raged in and between business and government buildings, the University of Huế, and the homes of 140,000 people. Catherine returned to document it. Before reaching Huế, evidence of the damage streamed down the road toward her. Refugees.

"Silent groups of children are walking towards us. We

Refugees flee the fighting in Saigon, Tết Offensive, February 1968.

Refugees brave crossfire in the hopes of finding safety at the Battle of Huế, Tét Offensive, February 1968.

are soon surrounded by hundreds of faces all full of hatred. Fingers are tightened onto my battledress; women and old men mumble insults echoed by the children; threatening fists rise up."

Huế came into view, a fiery skyline. As she approached, Catherine barely recognized it. "Bodies were strewn in the streets and [the] whole town was impregnated with a smell of putrefaction."

Raised above the old imperial palace waved the National Liberation Front flag. The devastated city lay trapped under the dense gray clouds of the monsoon. Nonstop sticky rain soaked it like a dirty rag.

Bombs had destroyed the bridge across the river that connected the new and old cities. Two-thirds of Huế's people lived in the neighborhoods of the old citadel. Its moat, and stone walls thirty feet high and more than twenty feet thick, proved no fortress against modern war machinery.

The US Marines had established a toehold inside the walls of the citadel and agreed to ferry Catherine and a group of journalists across the river. They entered through a gate into the Imperial City where the First Battalion, Fifth Marine Regiment had located a command post in a house. From there an escort led Catherine through the narrow streets to the First Battalion's B Company.

A US Marine advancing through Huế neighborhood, Tết Offensive, February 1968.

"The three hundred yards between us and the company seem interminable. Bodies of marines are strewn all over the place, covered in [ponchos]. One of them is stretched out in the middle of the road . . .

"[Another] dead marine is lying in the fetal position, he is wearing a silver wedding ring on his left hand."

B Company advanced into Hué on February 2, 197 men strong. Now, two weeks later, only 85 remained.

"The houses have been gutted and the street covered with rubble. On the ground are grenades, cartridge cases, several Viet and marine bodies mixed up among blood-sodden battle attire. A few yards farther along, a young marine is lying on a table in the middle of the street. At his sides, two friends are trying to comfort him."

"It's over, guys . . . I'm telling you, it's over . . ." The two marines protest energetically, but you can tell that they don't believe it themselves. The wounded marine took a whole AK-47 magazine in his belly a few moments earlier."

A few minutes more walking and Catherine reached the commander of B Company. He stood in the ruin of a house, shouting orders into the radio mic he gripped in his hand.

"The atmosphere is highly charged, everybody is insulting everybody else; some men have simply fallen to the ground, dazed by tiredness and lassitude . . . All are extremely dirty, their battle attire torn, covered with a growth of hair, and dripping in sweat."

By evening B Company regrouped and forged on. "The

worn-out marines don't speak, they walk like automatons with a slow and regular step, trying to avoid the rubble covering the street. Their worry is expressed only in silence." The strong carried the wounded into a house chosen as their base for the night. Catherine sat next to an injured man and spoke soothing words.

For the next six days, the men of B Company dodged sniper fire as they fought house-to-house toward the southeast wall of the citadel. As they exchanged fire with enemy soldiers, civilians scampered away, keeping their children close, searching for safety.

The marines battled yard by yard over burned ground, evacuating the casualties behind them. Catherine counted one marine killed for each block they advanced, one wounded for each house captured.

They needed air support, but heavy cloud cover hampered the bombers. Smoke from the burning rubble mixed with layers of misty fog; the nonstop drizzle drenched everything. When day turned to night, marines dropped to sleep without the strength to blow up their mattresses.

On February 21, B Company finally came within sight of the citadel's eastern wall. The command post ordered the men to advance.

"Then a miracle . . . For the first time in five days, the bombers are here. A North Vietnamese has just opened fire on one of them with an AK-47. We burst out laughing."

The laughter lasted only a moment. The men, eager, lit-

Men of US Marine Bravo Company, Battle of Huế, Tết Offensive, February 1968.

erally dying to win their objective, were ordered to fall back. They were too few for the job. B Company now numbered only fifty-three men. They were relieved by L Company of the Third Battalion, Fifth Marine Regiment, which took the southeast wall the following day. The battle for Huê continued ten more days.

Chapter 24

PHOTOS "FIRST CLASS"

Wednesday 6 March [19]68

Chère Maman,

. . . Black Star sent me a telegram to
say that the photos were "First Class" . . .
and <u>Look</u> cabled that the stuff was
fantastic . . .

My spirits are excellent. Warm hugs to
both of you . . .

Cath

Catherine returned to Saigon with her film from the Battle of Huế to find a *Life* magazine with her name on the front.

A color picture she'd taken of North Vietnamese soldiers filled the cover. The headline read "A Remarkable Day in Huế: the enemy lets me take his picture." And below that it said, "by Catherine Leroy."

Catherine's narrative of her capture and release spread over eight pages inside the magazine and included eleven photographs. The compassion that drove Catherine's work humanized the enemy soldiers, diverting from the image popular in the United States of crafty, evil Communist fighters. Her photos showed US Marines fighting to take back the city and the civilians caught in between.

Some colleagues said Catherine charmed her way to freedom, disparaging her courage, coolness under pressure, and that quality so vital to a good journalist: her desire to get the story.

Catherine's narrative of her capture and release was modest and matter-of-fact, giving most of the credit for their escape to François Mazure. She demonstrated none of the bravado and self-promotion often typical of male war photographers.

Shortly after Catherine saw her *Life* cover, she got word she had won the 1967 George Polk Award for news photography. She was to be awarded the Polk.

"My spirits are excellent," she wrote home. ". . . the George POLK award [is] the most important after [the] Pulitzer."

The Polk was awarded in nine categories honoring special achievement in journalism. Judges placed a premium on investigative work that was original, required digging and resourcefulness, and brought results. Catherine was recognized for depicting US Marines fighting at Đà Nẵng and the Navy corpsman trying to revive his dying buddy on Hill 881.

Though Catherine expressed excitement about her career success to her parents in private letters, she did not brag about it, and did not believe she demonstrated any particular courage.

"I always felt that it was a great privilege to be with the soldiers," she said. "To be accepted, to spend a couple of days or maybe a week with them. But I could leave any time, and they couldn't . . . To me, it was as if I [were] a deserter. Which is a bit ridiculous, but it's true."

Throughout the spring, President Johnson, his advisers and military leaders, scrambled to figure out what to do in

wide-eyed and hostile, and they pressed against us, pushing in from all sides. I was glad when a priest arrived—a good-looking Vietnamese of about 40, who spoke French with great elegance and precision. The wife of Bao Dai, the last emperor, had found refuge in this church, he told us, during a Viet Minh insurrection more than 20 years ago, and we were welcome to stay the night. The priest showed us around the cathedral and grounds. There were about 4,000 refugees, most of them women and children and old men. There were about 10 wounded, and one woman had just given birth to a baby. She lay on the floor in front of a confessional. Inside, the sound of all the people talking and the children crying was incredible, a rolling, continuous roar. That night we slept in the priest's room—or tried to. Next door in another room all the priests were praying loudly in Vietnamese, and their prayers were punctuated by bursts of gunfire.

Next morning, the priest told us flatly that the people were unhappy about our being there. They feared that our presence, as whites, might enrage the North Vietnamese. A young boy, a former juvenile delinquent with whom the priest had been working, volunteered to try to lead us through the North Vietnamese lines to the military compound where the Americans were holding out.

We left all our military clothes behind, even our boots. I got a pair of priest's sandals, François a pair of shower shoes. I stuffed my American and Vietnamese military identity cards in my bra along with several cans of film that were already exposed. I am only five feet tall and weigh 85 pounds, and I kept asking François, an old friend, "Look at my bosom. Does it look strange?" We made a white flag from one of the priest's robes, and made two big signs saying "Phap bao chi bale" and pinned them across our shirts. The priest himself wrote a letter for us in Vietnamese, explaining who we were. Then we started down the trail from the church, our young delinquent out ahead of us waving the white flag.

We soon came to a large, pleasant-looking villa with a garden around it, and suddenly

Caught in an enemy-held part of Hué, Cathy took shelter in a church crowded with hostile refugees (left). Nearby a mother lay with her baby (above).

we realized uniformed men were standing there staring at us. They looked astonished. The boy waved his white flag furiously, and we started shouting what was becoming our password—"Phap bao chi! Phap bao chi!"

Three men came up to us. They were North Vietnamese soldiers. They were dressed in khaki uniforms and carried AK-47 automatic rifles. Their faces were hostile, but they seemed calm. I was less afraid now than before. At least the three men were real—you could see them, smell them. They were somehow less frightening than the enemy with no face, the only one I had known before.

François handed them the letter from the priest. They looked at it but did not seem to be reading. They just stared at the paper. I saw François clutch his camera—the photographer's reflex was taking over. But the men took our cameras away and motioned to us to go ahead of them toward the garden. At the gate they tied our hands behind our backs with parachute cord. They were thorough rather than brutal.

When they led us into the garden, we saw about 15 soldiers sitting in foxholes dug under the trees. Several of them came up and looked at us im-

passively. François had retrieved the letter. He held it in his bound hands and each time a man came up to him he twisted around and presented the letter. "Mon Dieu," François said, "they aren't reading it! They just look at the paper."

We stood in the garden for about 45 minutes. François kept talking to them very angrily in French. In order not to seem frightened or apprehensive or guilty he acted as if he were offended and furious at being made to suffer such indignities. Overhead an American spotter plane and a Vietnamese bomber circled. Each time they came over, François and I dived for the dirt. The North Vietnamese seemed unconcerned—they hardly moved.

At last we were taken to a small building in back of the house, apparently the servants' quarters. When we walked in, we immediately saw a white man—heavy and about 50 years old with a worried face. "Are you French?" François burst out. "Yes, yes I am," the big man said. He seemed terribly glad to see us, and we were just as glad to see him. We even turned halfway around so that we could shake our bound hands. Almost nothing will stop a Frenchman from shaking hands.

The man told us an extraordinary story. He managed the

CONTINUED

The frowning North Vietnamese above balked at being photographed. But Cathy got this picture of him—with his captured U.S. military radio.

Behind the garden wall, two North Vietnamese pose with their Soviet-made weapons: a carbine (left) and grenade launcher (above). Below, the

North Vietnamese pretend to fire into a captured U.S. M-41 tank while Cathy reaches for a camera. Picture was taken by her colleague, François Mazure.

Life, February 16, 1968. Two of eight pages showing Catherine Leroy's exclusive photos and byline cover story telling of her capture and release by North Vietnamese soldiers amid the Battle of Huế, Tết Offensive. She appears on the left in the large picture (bottom) taken by her French colleague François Mazure.

Vietnam. Call up the reserves, ramp up the draft? Catherine continued to focus her lens on the realism of the war's toll on American boys and Vietnamese civilians alike.

Rising numbers of the American people could no longer stomach these pictures, nor bear the rising number of casualties. They could no longer find justification for this war. Protesters' voices had cried out against the United States' involvement in Vietnam for years. Now singular and influential people begin to question the wisdom and morality of sending Americans to die in Vietnam. Those condemning the war included Dr. Martin Luther King Jr., CBS News anchor Walter Cronkite, and renowned author and pediatrician Dr. Benjamin Spock.

After the week of bloodshed in Huế, Catherine took a break, decompressing in Hong Kong, then flying to New York to meet people in the news business and to accept her awards. Besides the George Polk, Catherine's work in 1967 was honored with the National Press Photographer Association's first prize in the news-report category, and the Sigma Delta Chi Award for news photography from the Society of Professional Journalists.

The announcement of the Robert Capa Award was a disappointment. The honor she had coveted went to another Vietnam War photographer, David Douglas Duncan. But she was invited to give an eight-minute speech at the Overseas Press Club gala, an event at the Hilton attended by a thousand people, including the US vice president, Hubert

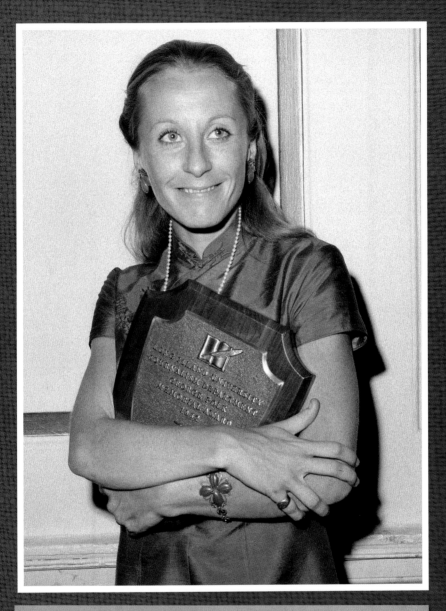

Catherine Leroy, 23, holding the George Polk Award she won for News Photography, April 1968, New York. Leroy was the first woman to receive the award and the first non-American. (AP Images)

Humphrey. Catherine wrote her mother later that week that she attended, "a big party with all the crème de la crème . . . where I'm supposed to smile the whole time."

Catherine dined with the head of her agency, Black Star, and made the rounds visiting editors at the agencies and magazines. On the evening of April 4, when Dr. Martin Luther King Jr. was assassinated, she happened to be in the New York offices of *Look* magazine, a major competitor of *Life*. When the staff at *Look* heard the news of King's death, the photo editor sent Catherine to photograph the reaction in Harlem, New York's predominately African American neighborhood. Violence erupted that night in cities across the country as many Black people tried to express their grief and anger at King's assassination.

Blond pigtails and cameras in hand, Catherine went to Harlem, her goal, as always, to get as close as possible. Almost immediately, she found herself surrounded by a hostile crowd. As the strain of the moment stretched toward a breaking point, a voice called out.

"Cathy, what are you doing here?"

Coming to her rescue was a former member of the 173rd Airborne Brigade, a marine with whom she'd made the parachute jump in Vietnam. The story goes, she got her

Catherine Leroy poses with two US Army soldiers while taking a break from patrolling South Vietnam's Central Highlands, circa 1967. (DCL)

photos and a home-cooked meal from the paratrooper's mother.

"Two days in Harlem. It's war there, too, no need to go to Vietnam," Catherine wrote her own mother. "Chère Maman, everything is OK. I'll call you. Big kisses, Cathy."

Visiting the states for nearly a month, Catherine realized she was more attached to Asia than she'd thought, missing the atmosphere, the colors, and the people. She hungered to get back to the war zone and returned to Vietnam and was soon chasing a new story, confident it had potential to land on the cover of *Life*.

"Lot of other journalists are on the list and once again I'll have to fight for it (but I'm afraid I must confess I like fighting . . . All fights and the excitement before and after them are worth it)."

AP correspondent Peter Arnett, who sometimes chased the same stories as Catherine, said after the war that competition between journalists for the different news outlets motivated them to risk danger.

"But that's what makes the American news world tick . . . that's what often pushed us into combat to a degree which in retrospect is remarkable, I suppose, maybe even foolish, but some stories you have to risk death to get. The overall impact of that reporting did come to terms with what was really happening, and the truth did out."

Chapter 25

THE BIGGEST HIGH OF ALL

Monday 9 September [1968]

   . . . I'm really afraid the war won't draw to a close for a long time yet . . .
   Cath

A Vietnamese woman holding wounded child in the midst of the deadly violence of the Battle of Huế, Tết Offensive, February 1968.

May 14, 1968, *Look* magazine published a powerful story featuring photographs Catherine had taken in Huế during the Tết Offensive. The story ran nine pages of her work chronicling the US Marines' harrowing advance on the citadel. She had written a diary of every hour as it played out. The article included Catherine's byline, her color photos, and text she wrote about her experience.

"The Americans here are boys of twenty, with the idealism of their age, but they are fighting a war without glory. They all look the same, from the First Cav to the US Marines, and they are united without discrimination by life and death."

Three of the six photos, stark with the cruel savagery and loss of life, covered full-spread pages of the magazine. One showed a marine facedown on the ground, his chest in a pool of blood. The caption: "I lose men," the commander said. "I lose so many men."

An editorial followed Catherine's photo essay in which the editors of *Look* claimed they had not published the photographs for the shock value, but as a reminder "that people

and nations make mistakes . . . and that in the process of recti-
fying a mistake, a person or a nation can grow in wisdom and
strength." *Look* followed *Time* and *Life* magazines, whose editorial stance had shifted to oppose the war in October 1967.
The *Look* editorial stated, "The Vietnam War has been a mistake, destroying something precious in the word *America*."

The editorial concluded, "We at *Look* believe that the
most important national business before us . . .is to wind up
our involvement in the Vietnam War as quickly and honorably as possible."

Catherine believed strongly in the power of photographs
as evidence. She continued to brave the battlefield with her
camera, always moving in as close as she could to act as a witness. Her pictures presented striking evidence of atrocious violence, unbearable suffering, deep compassion, and a magnitude of injustice at a crucial time when America was deeply
divided over whether the war was right or wrong.

United States soldiers would continue fighting in Vietnam for five more years, and the US would not extricate itself
from the war for two years after that. Catherine left at the end
of 1968. At age twenty-four, she'd proven herself an accomplished and highly regarded combat photographer. Three
years in Vietnam had been enough.

"I was not exactly well in my skin," Catherine said. "I was
extremely shell-shocked. It took years to get my head back
together, because I was filled with the sound of death, and
the smell of death." She felt an awful guilt leaving behind

young American soldiers she had "shot" in the field, knowing some would never leave Vietnam. And she carried much deeper emotional scars than those left by the physical wounds she'd suffered in the fight at Cồn Tiên.

Catherine made the United States her home, living in New York City and occasionally traveling to Paris. Her plans for a major documentary on the Vietnam War came to nothing due to a lack of funding, but in 1972, Catherine threw herself into a project that helped pull her from the darkness of post-traumatic stress after Vietnam.

She filmed and co-directed *Operation Last Patrol*, a documentary following a group of Vietnam veterans actively protesting the war. At peaceful anti-war demonstrations, some of the men were beaten by police and arrested numerous times. Wanting to make a big statement, hundreds of veterans caravanned from Los Angeles to Miami Beach, Florida, where the Republican Party was nominating President Richard Nixon for a second term. The film documented the veterans' demand that Nixon end the war and provide better health care to wounded vets.

That same year, Catherine carried her camera back into battle. She took an assignment to cover the escalating violence in Northern Ireland between Protestants and Catholic nationalists. Working for a French photo agency, she covered a military coup in Cyprus in 1974. And in early 1975 she went to Lebanon, a small country in the Middle East simmering with hostilities between Christians and Muslims.

Then, in March 1975, Catherine returned to Vietnam. For the prior ten months, the United States had been disengaging from the area, steadily withdrawing troops, and now hastily destroyed all remaining military hardware.

"I wanted to be there to see it happen much more than to be there for professional reasons . . . I had been very close to Vietnam and I wanted to see the end of it."

Catherine snapped photos, close-up, as North Vietnamese tanks clattered through the streets of Saigon. The last US personnel escaped, airlifting from the roof of the US Embassy.

As combat ended in Vietnam, civil war erupted in Lebanon. The press wanted pictures. Catherine caught a plane to Beirut.

"Absolutely, I wanted to be there," she said. "It's the biggest high of all, a massive rush of adrenaline. The high you experience in times of great danger is a high that you cannot experience anywhere else."

The following spring, Catherine's pictures of civil war in Lebanon won her the award she had coveted since her first year with a camera in Vietnam. The Overseas Press Club of America bestowed upon her in 1976 the prestigious Robert Capa Gold Medal. She was the first woman ever to win the award, which is given for the best published photographic reporting of the year that required exceptional courage and enterprise. The award was not necessary to attest that Catherine had gotten "close enough" to war. For a decade, her pictures had proven it.

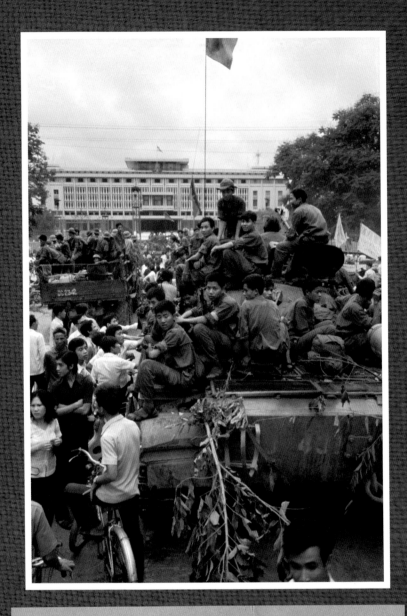

North Vietnamese and National Liberation Front of South Vietnamese soldiers and civilians in the streets of Saigon after the takeover of the presidential palace (in the background) as the last Americans escape and the city falls to the Communists, ending the war in Vietnam, April 25, 1975.

Epilogue

Time magazine offered Catherine a contract in 1977, and she worked for the news magazine up through the mid-1980s. The contract with *Time* guaranteed her a specific amount of work and income each month as she photographed war and strife around the world. Her assignments included the 1979 revolution in Iran and ongoing Middle East conflict in Libya, Egypt, Iraq, Jordan, and Gaza.

After five years covering the civil war in Lebanon, Catherine gathered her best photos of the ongoing conflict and the women and children caught in the crossfire. She published the book *God Cried* in collaboration with correspondent Tony Clifton, who covered the war in Lebanon for *Newsweek*.

Catherine went on to photograph violence in Afghanistan, Pakistan, and hot spots across Africa, including the civil war in Somalia.

"[Catherine] has a great news sense and an abiding desire to get where she wants to go," said Arnold Drapkin, *Time's* picture editor. "She's relentless when she wants something, and that's exactly what you want from a great newsperson. And of course, she always comes up with a marvelous image."

A portrait of Catherine Leroy taken during a photo shoot for *American Photography*'s cover story on Catherine's retirement from combat photography, December 1988 issue. (Jan Goossens)

One of Catherine's images earned her another major award in 1987, from the US National Press Photographers Association (NPPA). Her picture depicting the bombing of Tripoli in Libya was chosen picture of the year.

But after twenty years living and working in battle zones, Catherine grew weary. The job demanded so much of a person, in body, mind, and spirit. By the late 1980s, she had become sick of war, sick of taking pictures of conflict and its collateral damage. She retired from combat.

Despite her awards and many powerful images, she had remained relatively unknown. Partly because, despite her thirst for awards in her youth, she was humble about her work, always casting attention to other photographers she admired. In addition, as has long been true in our culture, women's work is often not valued as much as men's.

In 2005, Catherine published a book paying tribute to her colleagues from the Vietnam era, *Under Fire: Great Photographers and Writers in Vietnam*. The book paired images taken by the best photojournalists who covered the war with articles by journalists and writers who chronicled the conflict.

"We were never sure we would survive, or be able to translate it all into photographs that would have meaning," Catherine wrote in the introduction. "Yet there was no other place in the world we wanted to be. It mattered as if our lives depended on it. It did."

Whereas in earlier wars the actions of photographers and reporters had been tightly controlled by the military, the unparalleled freedom and access photographers and reporters experienced in Vietnam had been an experiment. Catherine said in her last public appearance, "I don't think it will be repeated."

Catherine shot a variety of peacetime assignments, including a carnival in Venice, modernization in China, and a day at work with Peter Jennings, a prime time ABC news anchor. One of her favorite jobs was photographing the Mohawk Indian "skywalkers," legendary ironworkers who built skyscrapers and bridges in New York City. She pursued her longtime love of fine clothing, traveling to Japan for a number of fashion shoots and starting a website business, Piece Unique, offering vintage haute couture.

Late in life, she became committed to the environment and the future of the planet. Catherine had seen the damage of massive bombings and defoliation in Vietnam. She put together a book proposal featuring photographs witnessing to the destruction of the environment through war and industrialization. No one was interested in publishing it.

Catherine had always loved the beach and settled finally in Los Angeles, where she lived with her cats. She enjoyed driving her black 1968 Mustang and the feel of the Pacific wind on her face. She passed away July 8, 2006, at the age of sixty-one.

Catherine believed a still photograph has more power than film or video. A picture captures a single moment in time, with the ability to impress it upon one's memory indelibly, to haunt even. She was motivated by a passionate hunger to seize singular moments when warfare collided with a human being, a man, woman, child, or enemy, and to preserve those moments so that we might look upon them and sense the connection we share.

Catherine said, "What I did was to give war a face.

"We are left with photography even more powerful today than when it captured the fractured moments of chaos. Now it's history."

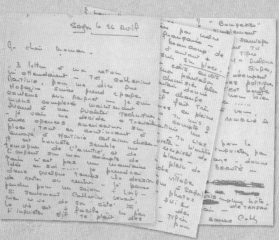

Catherine Leroy's letter to her mother from Vietnam, April 26, 1966.

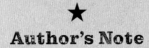

Author's Note

Throughout the years Catherine Leroy worked in Vietnam, she wrote letters regularly to her parents like the one shown opposite. In the 1960s, the high cost of international phone calls allowed for them only in emergencies. Nobody had a phone in their pocket. There was no email, text, or video calling. Letters were the common way families and friends kept in touch when they were apart.

Catherine's letters are what compelled me to write her story. It's not a book "about" Catherine Leroy. It is a deeply personal introduction to a courageous, passionate, and fallible young woman who sacrificed immeasurably to convey a story she believed was imperative for the world to understand.

Her words were personal, not meant for a future generation to read. At times you can see how, despite the magnitude of the work she was doing, she was still a very young woman in the process of maturing as an adult and finding her way where very few women had gone before. I was drawn by the naked ambition in her letters, the drive that fueled her success, as well as her doubts, tears, anger, and discouragement.

At the time Catherine went to Vietnam, I was beginning elementary school. Growing up, I, too, had ambitions of succeeding in the male-dominated career of journalism, in achieving my potential in a male-dominated world. The struggle was—and is—not easy. Often over the years, I have not found the confidence in myself that I see in Catherine.

Dear reader, I hope today you receive support for your dreams and have confidence in yourself. I hope Catherine's story of courage and perseverance will inspire you to take risks, believe in your potential, and do the hard work necessary to achieve your dreams. What you have to offer will make a difference in the world.

Catherine's story also demonstrates the unfortunate truth of how great purpose sometimes demands great price. Her photographs show us the human faces of war. Those faces haunted her for the rest of her life.

According to a friend of Catherine's, the violence and inhumanity of Vietnam alienated her from mainstream life in the same way many combat veterans are isolated in some form or another after returning from combat. She was filled with anxiety, smoked constantly, and became frighteningly thin. At times she was consumed by a ferocious anger at the hypocrisies of politics, other times filled with a sense of hopelessness, her eyes betraying a sort of fracture. She did not recognize—or maybe did not want to accept—that she suffered from post-traumatic stress disorder (PTSD).

When Catherine witnessed the United States going to war in Iraq and Afghanistan, she wanted Americans to heed lessons learned in Vietnam. She believed "people who knew war and photographed life in so many of its manifestations should be called upon by society to give their opinions on the future direction of the world. To at least play a part."

Living in Los Angeles in the summer of 2006, Catherine was diagnosed with lung and pancreatic cancer and died a week later on July 7. She was sixty-one. The Catherine Leroy Fund (Dotation Catherine Leroy or DCL) was founded in 2011 to preserve Catherine's work and provide a public archive of her materials.

I hope this book will also help carry on Catherine's legacy and her desire to make the world a better place.

How a Camera Worked in the 1960s

Cameras have changed dramatically since the time Catherine arrived in Vietnam. Today many of us use a cell phone to snap pictures of family and friends. A cell phone photo is created and stored digitally as long strings of numbers. The camera Catherine Leroy used worked much differently. It captured the light reflected off objects in the camera's field of view, then the light created a chemical reaction on film.

Film was a strip of flexible plastic, coated with a light-sensitive material, and wound onto the sprockets of a small spool. The spool of film came inside a light-proof cylinder that was loaded into the camera.

Cell phone cameras focus and adjust for light conditions automatically. You need only point and tap a finger. A burst function allows one tap to create dozens of photographs in seconds.

Catherine manually focused her camera, then depressed a button, which opened a shutter briefly, allowing light to enter through the lens. The light caused a chemical reaction that fixed an image on the film.

She used a setting on the camera to control how long the shutter stayed open, allowing in more or less light depending

A strip of 35 millimeter film after development.
(Prexels/Luriko Yamaguchi)

on conditions. This length of exposure and shutter speed varied by fractions of a second.

After taking each photo, Catherine pulled a lever with her thumb to advance the film, winding it onto the opposite spool. This slid a new piece of film across the aperture ready for the next shot. Pressing the button operated the shutter with a snapping sound, giving rise to the word *snapshot*.

When Catherine reached the end of a roll of film, twenty-four to thirty-six photos, she rewound it back into its canister, so as not to expose the film to light.

Developing the film required a darkroom, where the strip of film went through a series of chemical baths that revealed ghostly reverse images, or negatives, of what the photographer had seen. Further processing in the darkroom transferred images from the negatives onto paper, creating photographs.

Film being loaded into a 35 millimeter single-lens reflex camera. (Prexels/ekrulila)

Glossary

artillery—A class of heavy military weapons built to launch munitions far beyond the range and power of soldiers' rifles.

attrition—The act of using sustained attack or pressure to reduce the strength or effectiveness of someone or something.

B-52 Stratofortress—US long-range heavy bomber delivered for military service in 1955. First intended to be an atomic bomb carrier capable of reaching the Soviet Union, the B-52 was adapted for a number of different missions, including bombing North Vietnam during the Vietnam conflict. Dozens of B-52s remained in use by the US Air Force in the early twenty-first century.

battalion—A body of troops ready for battle consisting of four to six companies (tank or infantry) and may include up to 1,000 soldiers, usually commanded by a lieutenant colonel.

brigade—A brigade combat team consists of regiments or battalions of soldiers, including combat support (chemical warfare, combat engineering, intelligence, security, and communications) and combat service support (administration, maintenance, medical, supply, military police, training, cooks, chaplain) units necessary to sustain its operations.

Buddhist—A follower of Buddhism, the world's fourth-largest religion and a philosophy developed from the teachings of the Buddha—"awakened one" in Sanskrit—a man named Siddhartha Gautama who lived in northeastern India in the fifth century BCE.

C-130 Hercules—US military aircraft designed to transport troops and cargo, and make medical evacuations on crude runways in hostile areas. The C-130 has also been used as a gunship for airborne assault, search and rescue, aerial refueling, and firefighting.

captain—A military officer ranked above a lieutenant, usually commanding a company.

Claymore mines—Unlike conventional land mines, the Claymore was detonated by soldiers using remote control. Like a shotgun, the mine fired metal balls, which discharged in the direction of the target.

Cold War—A tense ideological conflict from 1946 to 1991 between the United States and the Soviet Union, characterized by an aggressive arms race, proxy wars, and rivalry for world dominance.

colonel—A senior military officer below the rank of general.

Communism—A political and economic system based on the theory of citizens' common ownership of property, means of production, and goods themselves. Communists propose that each person work according to his or her abilities and be paid according to need.

company—Consists of four platoons, commanded by a captain.

C ration—An amount of food supplied on a regular basis to US military ground forces in the field. C rations distributed in Vietnam during the war included one canned-meat item; one canned-fruit, bread, or dessert item; an accessory packet containing cigarettes, matches, chewing gum, toilet paper, coffee, cream, sugar, and salt; a single spoon; and one can opener for every three people.

corpsmen—Enlisted personnel trained to give first aid and carry off the wounded in combat, they deploy with both the US Navy and Marines.

demilitarized zone (DMZ)—A strip of land along the border between two countries in conflict where military weapons, activities, or personnel from both sides are forbidden by a treaty or other agreement.

Democratic Republic of Vietnam—Communist government established by Hồ Chí Minh in North Vietnam. Hồ formed the People's Army of Vietnam (PAVN).

Diệm, Ngô Đình—(January 3, 1901–November 2, 1963) A Vietnamese politician who was the final prime minister of the State of Vietnam, then served as president of South Vietnam from 1955 until he was deposed and assassinated during the 1963 military coup.

draft card—The Selective Service Act of 1917 required men of a certain age to register for military conscription to fill vacancies if there were not enough volunteers for the armed forces. "Draft card" was the colloquial name for the card given to show proof of registration. If a man's number was pulled in a draft lottery, he was sent a notice ordering him to report for duty.

F-4 Phantom II—Two-seat, twin-engine, long-range supersonic fighter-bomber and jet interceptor used by the US Navy beginning in 1960 and later used by the US Marine Corps and US Air Force.

First Cavalry—The First Cavalry Division based at Fort Hood, Texas, is one of the most decorated combat divisions of the US Army. Since its formation in 1921, its members have served in every American conflict from World War II to the present day. The last mounted troopers of the First Cavalry Division traded their horses for jeeps, trucks, and tanks in 1943 to fight the Japanese in World War II.

flak jacket—Jacket- or vest-style body armor designed to protect soldiers from shrapnel from high-explosive weaponry such as antiaircraft artillery, grenades, and antipersonnel mines. Not designed to protect against bullets from rifles or handguns.

French Foreign Legion—Comprising a branch of the French Army unique in accepting foreign recruits, legionnaires are highly trained special-forces infantry soldiers.

general—A high-ranking military officer, the commander of an army. There are different ranks of general, such as general, lieutenant general, brigadier general, major general. In this book I have used full titles at first reference and then simply "general."

Geneva Conference (1954)—The meeting to decide the future of the former French colony of Indochina after the French surrender to the Việt Minh at Điện Biên Phủ. At issue: extricating France from East Asia, the stabilization of Laos and Cambodia, and the unification of Vietnam.

The conference included representatives from France, the Democratic Republic of Vietnam (Communist Việt Minh), the Republic of South Vietnam (democratic, as recognized by the United States), China, the Soviet Union, Laos, Cambodia, and the United States.

An agreement was reached to divide Vietnam in half along the seventeenth parallel, with the Việt Minh controlling the northern section and the Republic of Vietnam the south. General elections would take place in both north and south on July 20, 1956, to decide which Vietnam would govern the whole country.

The Việt Minh, under the leadership of Hồ Chí Minh, occupied significant territory south of the seventeenth parallel. They agreed to withdraw, believing they would be voted into power in the coming elections. Fearing that this was true, the United States did not sign the agreement.

GI—Originally the acronym for "galvanized iron," which was stamped on US Army garbage cans, it came to stand for "government issue," describing US military equipment and now generally used to refer to a foot soldier.

grenade—A small explosive weapon triggered by a firing pin and usually thrown by hand. Can also refer to an explosive shot from a grenade launcher.

guerilla—A member of a small group of fighters typically confronting a larger, less mobile, traditional military and using irregular tactics including ambushes, sabotage raids, and hit-and-run attacks.

hamlet—A small village.

Hồ Chí Minh—(Born Nguyen Sinh Cung; May 19, 1890–September 2, 1969) Revolutionary and prime minister and president of the Democratic Republic of Vietnam who commanded the Communist North Vietnamese (Việt Minh) forces during the Vietnam War.

"Huey"—Bell UH-1 Iroquois US Army helicopter, the most common utility chopper used in the Vietnam War for carrying troops and evacuating wounded. It was not fitted with external weapons but armed with door gunners and nicknamed "Huey" due to its initial HU-1 designation.

infantry—Soldiers fighting on foot.

Iwo Jima—The Battle of Iwo Jima saw some of the most brutal fighting of World War II; it pitted US Marines against the Imperial Army of Japan in early 1945 on the small Pacific island.

land mine—An explosive device concealed under or on the ground that detonates automatically when a person steps on it or a vehicle drives over it.

leathernecks—Nickname for US Marines, thought to stem from the leather collar on early uniforms that resulted in a straight-necked posture.

lieutenant—Lowest-ranking military officer, commands a platoon.

marines—The Marine Corps, one of the United States' eight military services, originated in 1775 in Philadelphia with the formation of the Continental Marines, two battalions of infantry troops to fight on both land and sea. Today the marines conduct expeditionary and amphibious operations with the US Navy, Army, and Air Force.

mercenary—A soldier of fortune; a professional soldier hired in a foreign army who fights for money or other payment.

monsoon—A seasonal shift in wind direction and air pressure that often causes heavy rain.

mortar—A short-barreled, mobile weapon that fires an explosive shell, or solid shot, at a high trajectory for a short distance.

napalm—A highly flammable mixture of a gelling agent and a volatile petrochemical, used in bombs and flamethrowers, burns at extremely high temperatures, sticks to foliage and human skin, and is difficult to extinguish.

National Liberation Front of South Vietnam—Communist-organized armed resistance movement in South Vietnam. Its members and guerrilla fighters were called the derogatory name Việt Cộng by the Americans.

ordnance—Military supplies including weapons, ammunition, combat vehicles, and maintenance tools and equipment.

pacification—US policy during the Vietnam War designed to protect civilians from guerilla rebel violence and assist in maintaining political and economic stability in rural areas, it usually consisted of programs attempting to win the "hearts and minds" of the Vietnamese people and counter the Communist insurgency.

paratrooper—A soldier trained to attack after parachuting from an aircraft.

platoon—A military unit consisting of forty-two to fifty-five infantry soldiers, divided into three or four squads of up to twelve soldiers each, and commanded by a lieutenant.

post-traumatic stress disorder (PTSD)—Once called shell shock or battle fatigue, PTSD is a mental health condition affecting people who have experienced or witnessed profound emotional trauma such as military combat, torture, or natural disaster. Symptoms may include recurrent flashbacks, nightmares, severe anxiety, eating disorders, fatigue, and social withdrawal, as well as uncontrollable thoughts about the stressful event.

Pulitzer Prize—An award for achievements in newspaper, magazine, or online journalism, literature, and musical composition that taps the current pulse of popular and literary American conscience.

quagmire—A sticky situation that is difficult to get out of, such as trying to pull your foot from deep mud.

radioman—A military enlisted person specializing in communications and responsible for receiving and transmitting radio signals and information from headquarters to the field and vice versa.

rank—A system of hierarchical relationships in military forces; degrees of leadership and responsibility for personnel, equipment, and mission grow with each increase in rank.

regiment—A unit of army soldiers commanded by a colonel, often consisting of four battalions.

Republic of South Vietnam—Purported democracy established in the southern city of Saigon, supported by the United States, which sent money and military advisers to organize and train South Vietnamese military forces, called the Army of the Republic of Vietnam (ARVN).

rickshaw—A light, two-wheeled covered vehicle, drawn by a cyclist with a seat for one or two passengers behind the driver.

rocket—A self-propelled explosive charge that increases speed during flight and explodes upon landing; more powerful than the mortar.

Roman Catholic Church—Worldwide Christian church in communion with the pope in Rome.

Sarge—Short for "sergeant," the leader of a squad of twelve enlisted soldiers.

shell—Originally a "bombshell," an explosive projectile fired from a cannon, howitzer, mortar, etc.

shrapnel—Lead balls or fragments of a bomb, shell, or other object thrown off by its explosion.

telegram—A written message sent and received via electrical impulses sent by wire or other communications channel.

telephoto lens—A camera lens with a longer focal length than standard that allows one to zoom in to photograph a distant subject without compromising picture quality.

teleprinter—An electromechanical device that produces hard-copy messages from signals received via telephone lines, satellites, or a radio relay system. A keyboard transmitter turns a typed message into coded pulses that are transmitted to a receiver that converts incoming signals to letters and words and prints out the message.

United Service Organizations (USO)—The organization that sends entertainers to perform for military troops for the purpose of boosting morale.

Việt Cộng—A derogatory name Americans called the rebel soldiers of the National Liberation Front of South Vietnam, it is an organized Communist group whose members used guerrilla tactics to resist the government of South Vietnam.

Việt Minh—Followers of Communist leader Hồ Chí Minh, including the North Vietnamese Army.

Timeline

August 27, 1944: Catherine Leroy is born in Sannois, France.

September 2, 1945: The Vietnamese claim independence. When Japan surrenders, ending World War II, Hồ Chí Minh establishes the Democratic Republic of Vietnam, Hà Nội as its capital, and himself president. Nevertheless, no other countries acknowledge this government. French troops reoccupy Vietnam, leading to war between the French and the Việt Minh.

May 7, 1954: France surrenders colony of Indochina. French forces capitulate to the Việt Minh after suffering a decisive defeat at Điện Biên Phủ.

July 1954: The Geneva Accords divide Vietnam. The Geneva Conference negotiates an armistice for the peaceful withdrawal of French troops from Vietnam and temporarily divides Vietnam at the seventeenth parallel, with a provision for general elections to reunify the country in 1956.

1955: With support from the United States, Ngô Đình Diệm proclaims the Republic of South Vietnam, with himself president in Saigon.

March 1965: First American troops arrive and bombing begins in Vietnam; 3,500 US Marines land near Da Nang, South Vietnam. US bombing of North Vietnam, called Operation Rolling Thunder, continues from 1965 to 1968.

February 1966: Catherine Leroy arrives in Vietnam.

August 27, 1966: Catherine celebrates her twenty-second birthday with US Marines at Da Nang, South Vietnam.

September 1966: The First Cavalry Division launches Operation Thayer, a massive air assault, in Bong Son Plain, three hundred miles northeast of Saigon. Catherine rides in the third helicopter in the first assault wave.

February 22, 1967: Catherine parachutes into combat. Joining the 173rd Airborne Brigade in Operation Junction City, Catherine becomes the first female to jump into combat with American paratroopers.

May 1967: Catherine photographs the battle for Hill 881. Catherine's series of photos of Navy corpsman Vernon Wike going to the aid of his dying friend would become her most renowned.

May 1967: Catherine is evacuated to the USS *Sanctuary* after being caught in a mortar blast and injured by more than thirty pieces of shrapnel during Operation Hickory at Cồn Tiên.

October 1967: A single protest of the Vietnam War draws one hundred thousand participants. Antiwar demonstrations in the United States had increased in size and frequency in 1967. During this event at the Lincoln Memorial in Washington, DC, some protesters broke away to illegally march on the Pentagon, the first major act of nonviolent civil disobedience in objection to the war.

January 30, 1968: The Tết Offensive, a surprise attack during the Vietnamese New Year holiday of Tết, begins. North Vietnamese and PLAF forces assault five major cities, the US Embassy in Saigon, dozens of military installations, and scores of towns and villages throughout South Vietnam.

January 31, 1968: Catherine is captured by enemy soldiers in the first days of the Battle of Huế. She convinces the North Vietnamese to release her. Her photographs and story, "A Remarkable Day in Huế: The enemy lets me take his picture," makes the front cover of *Life* magazine.

March 1968: Catherine wins the George Polk Award for news photography, the first woman to do so. Her work from the past year also won the National Press Photographer Association's first prize and the Sigma Delta Chi Award for news photography from the Society of Professional Journalists.

Early 1969: Catherine leaves Vietnam. She continues to photograph for major newspapers and magazines, covering conflicts around the world; she would spend more than ten years in the Middle East.

April 29, 1975: The US war in Vietnam ends. All remaining American personnel make emergency evacuations from Saigon as North Vietnamese troops march toward the city. Anticipating events, Catherine returns to document the fall of Saigon while most Western journalists leave the country. The South Vietnamese government surrenders unconditionally the following day.

1976: Catherine wins the Robert Capa Gold Medal, becoming the first woman to secure this prestigious award from the Overseas Press Club of America.

1987: Catherine wins Picture of the Year prize from the US National Press Photographers Association for her photograph of the bombing in Tripoli, Libya.

2006: Catherine dies of lung and pancreatic cancer at sixty in Los Angeles, California.

Notes

Chapter 1

1   "Vientiane, Laos, February 1966 . . . Catherine." All excerpts of letters from Catherine Leroy to her mother, Denise Leroy, and father, Jean Leroy: archive, Dotation Catherine Leroy, Paris, France.

3   "I want to become . . . the Vietnam War." Catherine Leroy, *Vietnam Narrative*, translated by Sotires Eleftheriou (unpublished manuscript, received December 13, 2019), PDF, Dotation Catherine Leroy, Paris, France, 1.

Chapter 2

15–16   "Helicopters swarmed . . . steel wasps." Geoffrey C. Ward and Ken Burns, *The Vietnam War: An Intimate History* (New York: Penguin Random House, 2017), 149.

19   "I practically . . . I wanted to do." Peter Howe, "The Death of a Fighter: Catherine Leroy, 1944–2006." *Digital Journalist*, August 2006, digitaljournalist.org/issue0608/the-death-of-a-fighter.html.

19   "Photojournalists were my heroes." Donald R. Winslow, "Vietnam War Photojournalist Catherine Leroy, 60," July 11, 2006, accessed July 8, 2020, nppa.org/news/2168.

Chapter 3

26   "You get used to it . . . change often here." C. Leroy to D. Leroy, February 26/27, 1966.

27   "frenetic agitation . . . minute of the day." Leroy, *Narrative*, 2.

32   "She was a timid . . . another one." Horst Faas. *Horst Faas on Catherine Leroy*, filmed March 1, 2011, Munich, Germany, accessed September 13, 2018, vimeo.com/104250338.

32   "You have experience . . . Yes, she lied." Carol Squiers, "Catherine Leroy," *American Photography*, December 1988, 35.

32   "If you can get anything . . . a picture." Ibid.

32–33   "I was a child . . . and I went." Howe, "Death of."

Chapter 4

36   "We make a pleasant . . . work with them." C. Leroy to D. Leroy, 8 April 1966.

36–37   "I've become a great . . . any qualms." Ibid.

37	"She cried in her heart." Jaqueline Demornez, "Vietnam: Catherine Leroy une petite Française de 23 ans étonne les Américains," *Elle*, May 13, 1968, 80.
38	"I was always kicked . . . to run away." Demornez, "Vietnam," 80–81.
38	"I was a very difficult . . . of my mind." Peter Howe, *Shooting Under Fire: The World of the War Photographer* (New York: Artisan, 2002), 107.
38–39	"Tired of selling wind." Demornez, "Vietnam," 80–81.
39	"I was a gifted . . . very big challenge." Howe, *Shooting Under*, 107.

Chapter 5

50	"As a woman . . . bore me stiff." C. Leroy to D. Leroy, 8 April 1966.
52	"You can't come . . . have changed." *Faas on Catherine Leroy*.
53	"I'm not so self-conscious . . . skills anymore." C. Leroy to D. Leroy, 26 April 1966.

Chapter 6

57	"And I would jump . . . had no effect." Leroy, *Narrative*, 2.
58	"Instead of me . . . lowest level." James R. Chiles, *The God Machine: From Boomerangs to Black Hawks, the Story of the Helicopter* (New York: Bantam Dell Random House, 2007), 170.
58	"Moving like ghosts . . . and minimum rations." Ibid., 170.
58	"We went out . . . then water." Ibid., 170.
59	"The men I discovered . . . weary gestures." Leroy, *Narrative*, 2.
61	"I didn't look like them, they did not accept me." Ibid., 2.
61	"In the near future . . . awhile longer." C. Leroy to D. Leroy, 26 April [1966].
61	"It is unthinkable not . . . four or five." C. Leroy to D. Leroy, 8 April 1966.

Chapter 7

70	"I'm Captain Bird . . . care of you." Leroy, *Narrative*, 3.
71	"I have to learn . . . place my foot." Ibid., 3.
71	"I'm tired out by . . . no strength." Leroy, *Narrative*, 4.

Chapter 8

76	"Aren't you ashamed? . . . lucky you are?" Leroy, *Narrative*, 3.
76	"It's difficult . . . about you." Ibid., 4.
77	"At night I sleep . . . been adopted." Ibid., 7.
80	"Thousands of rickshaws . . . young Vietnamese." Ibid., 5.
80	"Painfully pushing the sticky air . . ." Ibid., 7.

Chapter 9

85–86   "The Huey suddenly . . . the undergrowth." Leroy, *Narrative*, 7.

86–87   "Everything happens . . . Get out . . . Get out . . ." Ibid., 7.

87   "Horrible stomach cramp . . . the sergeant." Ibid., 7.

87   "Are you OK? Not too scared?" Ibid., 8.

87   "I'm out of breath . . . gone cramped again." Ibid., 8.

90   "The gunships are coming . . . of the Viets." Ibid., 8.

90   "The rockets tear . . . enormous clouds of dust." Ibid., 8.

90   "On the surface . . . thirty hours straight." Howe, *Shooting Under*,101.

90   "Everybody, food . . ." Ibid., 8.

91   "I always felt . . . food was nice." Susan A. Freudenheim, "A window on
        the war," *Los Angeles Times*, December 8, 2002, latimes.com/archives/
        la-xpm-2002-dec-08-ca-freudenheim8-story.html.

Chapter 10

95   "How old are you?" And continuing conversation with officer. Leroy, *Nar-
        rative*, 8.

99   "Compassion . . . anything but subjective." Steven Winn, "What can
        photos teach us about war? Have a look," *San Francisco Chronicle*, April
        19, 2005, sfgate.com/entertainment/article/What-can-photos-teach-us-
        about-war-Have-a-look-2678825.php.

99   "Do you think they can . . . all these . . ." Ibid., 10.

99   "Given by their American friends." Ibid., 9.

101   "Clumsily bandaged . . . (including all doctor's comments) . . . again
        tomorrow." Ibid., 9.

101–102 "Anything that moves . . . area is a potential friend." Benis M. Frank,
        "Lieutenant General Victor H. Krulak, USMC (Retired)," interviewed
        by Benis M. Frank, US Department of the Navy, Historical Division, US
        Marine Corps, Washington, DC, 1973, 26, usmcu.edu/Portals/218/
        LtGen%20Victor%20H_%20Krulak.pdf.

102   "Basically, I kept insisting . . . *he cannot win*." John C. McManus, *Grunts:
        Inside the American Infantry Combat Experience, World War II Through
        Iraq* (New York: Penguin Publishing Group, 2010), 208.

102   "I saw it as . . . successful outcome." Ibid., 208.

102   "When will it be finished?" All General Krulak's comments. Leroy,
        Narrative, 9.

102   "The soup is ready . . . to be given soup." Ibid., 10.

Chapter 11

109   "I was so scared sometimes . . . very primal." Howe, "Death of," Digital Journalist, August 2006, digitaljournalist.org/issue0608/the-death-of-a-fighter.html.

111   "Friendship, camaraderie . . . masks." Ibid.

111   "Her pictures reflect . . . impossible feat." Ibid.

111–112 "Who roam untiringly . . . five cameras." Leroy, *Narrative*, 7.

112   "She's a tiny *mouche* . . . with a picture." Freudenheim, "A window."

114   "For a war photo . . . with sensitivity." Catherine Leroy, interviewed by Marcel Giuglaris, March 7, 1968. dotationcatherineleroy.org/en/interviews1/with-catherine-leroy, accessed October 27, 2020.

Chapter 12

119   "Rice paddies . . . likely to be shot at." C. Leroy to D. Leroy, 24 January [1966].

119   "Water . . . watching soldiers." Leroy, *Narrative*, 12.

119   "Marching for unending . . . and tiredness." Ibid., 12.

119–120 "The jungle, the jungle . . . great fun!!!!" C. Leroy to D. Leroy, 25 August [19]67.

120   "The marines are really great . . . war medals. C. Leroy to D. Leroy, 13 July [1966].

120   "Wait a minute . . . boot is caught." Stella Pope Duarte, "I never mourned Vietnam." *Latino Perspectives Magazine*, November 1 2010, latinopm.com/opinion/voices/ps/i-never-mourned-vietnam-4390#.XtWEfDpKiM8.

120   "I had a nice time . . . on my plate." C. Leroy to D. Leroy, 9 September [1968].

121   "In Vietnam, most of . . . break loose." Freudenheim, "A window."

121   "Always being on the lookout . . . get discouraged." Leroy, *Narrative*, 12.

123   "Work is tough . . . out of the country." C. Leroy to D. Leroy, 13 July [19]66.

123   "It's been going on . . . good faith." C. Leroy to J. Leroy, 1 December 1966.

123   "Got back yesterday . . . at the moment." C. Leroy to D. Leroy, 15 November 1966.

123   "I'll send a few photos to . . . one day." Ibid.

125   "A letter from Black . . . Urgent . . ." Ibid., 21 December [1966].

126   "I'm jumping . . . 101st Airborne." Ibid.

Chapter 13

132 "We own the day, but [the enemy] owns the night." Source unknown.

133 "The Viets don't let . . . contain much good." C. Leroy to D. Leroy, 24 January 1967.

134 "It is easier . . . Pulitzer Prize." Ibid.

135 "I've just had the . . . my parachute jump." Ibid., 9 February 1967.

135 "Amazing capacity to . . . and yet jumped." Robert Pledge interviewed by the author, October 14, 2019.

135 "Was an enormous . . . I wasn't a coward." Squiers, *Catherine Leroy*, 35.

Chapter 14

140 "You end up going a bit crazy." C. Leroy to D. Leroy, 19 February 1967.

140 "At least one week . . . charming people." C. Leroy to D. Leroy, 24 January 1967.

140 "It's all a matter of luck . . . at my age?" Ibid.

141 "Orders barked . . . more banks." Leroy, *Narrative*, 13.

143–144 "A number of soldiers . . . obeys him." Ibid.

144 "It's extremely rare . . . the last month." C. Leroy to D. Leroy, 8 March 1967.

144 "Both we and the . . . our rifles." Philip Caputo, *A Rumor of War: The Classic Vietnam Memoir* (New York: Picador Henry Holt and Company, 2017), 228.

144–146 "Life is plentiful, life is cheap in the Orient." Derrick Z. Jackson, "The Westmoreland mind-set," *New York Times*, July 22, 2005, nytimes.com/2005/07/22/opinion/derrick-z-jackson-the-westmoreland-mindset.html.

Chapter 15

151 "Do you still want to [jump]?" Leroy, *Narrative*, 14.

151 "Guys, we're going . . . in North Vietnam." Leroy, *Narrative*, 14.

152 "We'll be the first to jump [in Vietnam]." Ibid.

152 "Small and thin . . . be blown away." Alice Gabriner, ed., "'Who Is the Enemy Here?' The Vietnam War Pictures That Moved Them Most." Undated photo essay, *Time*, time.com/vietnam-photos, accessed July 2, 2020.

153 "The men were all quiet . . . we reached the dropping zone." Leroy, *Narrative*, 14.

153 "Let's go . . . Let's go . . ." Ibid., 14.

153 "I had butterflies . . . landing zone." Ibid., 14.

155 "I'm very proud . . . into a tree." Freudenheim, "A window."

155   "Where's Catherine . . . over there now." Leroy, *Narrative*, 15.

155   "That was your eighty-fifth jump. Wear it." Ibid., 15.

156   "I've made over four thousand francs . . . lots of dresses . . ." C. Leroy to D. Leroy, 5 March 1967.

156–157 "I was supposed . . . I never gave in." C. Leroy to J. Leroy, 23 February 1967.

Chapter 16

161   "Don't worry, everything is fine." C. Leroy to D. Leroy, 26 February 1967.

161   "I wear it on my battle . . . green with envy." C. Leroy to D. Leroy, 8 March 1967.

161   "Many were very . . . chauvinistic pigs." Elizabeth Herman, "In Her Own Words, Photographing the Vietnam War," *New York Times*, September 27, 2017, lens.blogs.nytimes.com/2017/09/27/in-her-own-words-photographing-the-vietnam-war/.

162   "It was not a man . . . to a grasshopper." Michèle Ray, *The Two Shores of Hell* (London: Murray, 1967), 30.

162   "I think probably she couldn't think . . . I know it was." Jonathan Randal, "The Hill Fights, Khe Sanh, April–May 1967," excerpt from *Cathy at War*, vimeo.com/201391788, accessed September 13, 2018.

163   "Oh, I'd love to go with you . . . It was ridiculous." Freudenheim, "A window."

163   "Without her press card . . . that was a problem." Christian Simonpiétri, "Christian Simonpiétri on Catherine Leroy, Paris, France, March 16, 2012," vimeo.com/104023209, accessed July 8, 2020.

164   "She had a tendency . . . they told me so." Don McCullin, "Don McCullin on Catherine Leroy, Paris, France, March 17, 2012," vimeo.com/104013791, accessed September 13, 2018.

164   "A few people are . . . they're all b–s." C. Leroy to D. Leroy, 10 April 1967.

164   "She was a legend . . . combat she saw." Freudenheim, "A window."

164–165 "Catherine was a tough cookie . . . kindly with fools." Donald R. Winslow, *Vietnam War Photojournalist Catherine Leroy, 60*, July 11, 2006, nppa.org/news/2168, accessed July 8, 2020.

165   "I never really had any trouble . . ." Howe, "Death of."

167   "Horst Faas tells . . . out of luck." C. Leroy to D. Leroy, 27 March 1967.

167–168 "I had thought . . . I cried all morning." C. Leroy to D. Leroy, 27 March 1967.

168   "I've bought you . . . think about you." C. Leroy to D. Leroy, 2 November 1966.

168   "I've just bought . . . to the ground." C. Leroy to D. Leroy, 10 April 1967.

168   "Newest thing . . . bored in Saigon." C. Leroy to D. Leroy, 11 April 1967.

Chapter 17

172   "I went there for a feature . . . being on vacation." Leroy, *Narrative*, 15.

172–173 "All of them were killed . . . off your headband." Leroy, *Narrative*, 15.

175   "I don't think she was . . . getting the shots." Robert Pledge interviewed by the author, October 14, 2019.

176   "There was no way . . . after they were dead." Arnold Blumberg, "The First Battle of Khe Sahn," undated, historynet.com/first-battle-khe-sahn.htm, accessed July 8, 2020.

176   "Grappling in hand-to-hand with the hillside." Leroy, *Narrative*, 15.

176–177 "Climbing past the bodies . . . napalm and bombing." Catherine Leroy, "The Hill Fights, Khe Sanh, April–May 1967," excerpt from *Cathy at War*, vimeo.com/201391788, accessed September 13, 2018.

177   "A marine falls . . . automatic gunfire." Leroy, *Narrative*, 15.

177   "I heard a bang . . . didn't have a chance." Jeffrey Elbies, "They Were Soldiers Once," *Popular Photography*, December 17, 2008, popphoto.com/how-to/2008/12/they-were-soldiers-once/, accessed September 12, 2018.

Chapter 18

183   "Blasted jungle . . . that they were new." Horst Faas," The Hill Fights, Khe Sanh, April–May 1967," excerpt from *Cathy at War*, vimeo.com/201391788, accessed September 13, 2018.

184   "She went thinking . . . volunteer to be there." Pledge, October 14, 2019.

187   "The pictures I took . . . in Vietnam for." James Macardle, *On This Date in Photography*, August 27, 2017, onthisdateinphotography.com/2017/08/27/august-27/, accessed July 8, 2020.

190   "But where were you? I didn't see you." Leroy, *Narrative*, 16.

190   "I am very happy . . . and see us soon." Ibid., 16.

190   "Chère Maman . . . stuck in the village of Khe Sanh." C. Leroy to D. Leroy, 12 May 1967.

190   "[I am the] first . . . (since Horst Faas in 1965)." C. Leroy to D. Leroy, 13 May 1967.

191   "*Time* said my photos . . . end of the year." C. Leroy to D. Leroy, 12 May 1967.

191   "I've made a name for myself . . . getting what I want." C. Leroy to D. Leroy, 7 May 1967.

191   "I mean, who was I . . . such terrific work." Jonathan Randal, "The Hill Fights, Khe Sanh, April–May 1967," excerpt from *Cathy at War*, vimeo. com/201391788, accessed September 13, 2018.

Chapter 19

194–195 "A young marine . . . be amputated." Leroy, *Narrative*, 17.

195   "Incoming . . . Incoming . . ." Ibid., 17.

198   "We were being mortared . . . there is only blood." Ibid., 17.

198   "I think she's dead, Sarge." Tony Clifton, "Catherine Leroy: French photographer whose images charted the horror of war from Vietnam to Beirut," *The Guardian*, July 20, 2006, theguardian.com/news/2006/ jul/21/guardianobituaries.france, accessed July 8, 2020.

Chapter 20

202   "Now, now . . . this is hardly the time to be modest." Leroy, *Narrative*, 17.

203   "She won't make it . . ." Ibid., 17.

206   "My God! A woman . . . a blonde." Ibid., 18.

206   "It's nothing . . . pretty French woman." Ibid., 18.

207   "I can't give you a Purple Heart . . . use for this." Ibid., 18.

209   "Vacant and wearing . . . euphoric." Ibid., 18.

209   "The scar on my cheek . . . wear my dresses." C. Leroy to D. Leroy, June 1967.

209–210 "I want to come . . . Robert Capa prize." C. Leroy to D. Leroy, 23 June 1967.

210   "Chère Maman . . . each other again." Ibid.

Chapter 21

214   "Inside the command. . . bite the marines." Leroy, *Narrative*, 19.

215   "My stay in New York . . . green with envy." C. Leroy to D. Leroy, 15 November [1967].

219   "I had brought . . . to use the bikini." Freudenheim, "A window."

Chapter 22

223   "I've been told . . ." and all conversation with Marine Charlie McMahon. Charlie McMahon, "Charlie McMahon Oral History Interview on the Vietnam War," *Witness to War*, C-SPAN 3, May 20, 2018, c-span.org/ video/?445353-2/charlie-mcmahon-oral-history-interview-viet-nam-war.

223   "We were growing nervous . . ." and all Leroy quotes about her time in Huế, *Catherine Leroy*, "A Remarkable Day in Huế: The enemy lets me take his picture," *Life*, February 16, 1968, 22-29.

226   "The people did not look . . . from all sides." Ibid., 22–24.

226   "There were about ten wounded . . . continous roar." Ibid., 24.

227   "I am only five . . . Does it look strange?'" Ibid., 24.

227   "Pháp báo chí từ . . . Paris." Ibid., 24.

227–230 "Their faces were hostile . . . had known before." Ibid., 24.

230   "I had seen many . . . in front of me." Leroy, "A Remarkable Day," 2.

231   "We said that we had . . . file our report." Howe, *Shooting Under Fire*. 105.

231   "He seemed very pleased . . . in the American units." Leroy, "A Remarkable Day," 26.

231   "Phony heroic poses." Ibid., 26.

231   "I thought it was . . . been in the news." Leroy, interviewed by Giuglaris.

231   "I doubt that . . . a victorious army." Leroy, "A Remarkable Day," 26.

231   "But I was so scared . . . brilliant photojournalist." Howe, *Shooting Under Fire*, 105.

232   "Well, we have to get back to Paris with our story," he said, "so we'll be running along now." Leroy, "A Remarkable Day," 26.

232   "François," Catherine said and said again, "I'll kiss the first two Americans I meet!" Leroy, "A Remarkable Day," 28.

233   "There are four thousand refugees in there," she yelled. "They aren't VC, they are just people!" Ibid., 28.

Chapter 23

236–240 "Silent groups of children . . . fists rise up." Leroy, *Narrative*, 24.

240   "Bodies were strewn . . . putrefaction." Ibid., 25.

242   "The three hundred yards . . . his left hand." Ibid., 26.

242   "The houses have . . . a few moments earlier." Ibid., 26.

242   "The atmosphere is . . . dripping in sweat." Ibid., 26–27.

242–243 "The worn-out . . . only in silence." Ibid., 27.

243   "Then a miracle . . . burst out laughing." Ibid., 33.

Chapter 24

249   "My spirits are excellent . . . after the Pulitzer." C. Leroy to D. Leroy, 6 March 1968.

249   "I always felt . . . but it's true." Freudenheim, "A window."

255   "Cathy, what are you doing here?" Winslow, "Vietnam War Photojournalist."

256   "Two days in Harlem . . . Big kisses, Cathy." C. Leroy to D. Leroy, 8 April 1968.

256   "Lot of other journalists . . . worth it)." C. Leroy to D. Leroy, 27 September 1968.

256   "But that's what makes . . . the truth did out." Peter Arnett, "Witness to War: Pulitzer Prize Winning Reporter Peter Arnett Talks About His Years in Vietnam." youtube.com/watch?v=e3DJiSO9MhI, accessed 11/13/2020.

Chapter 25

261   "The Americans here . . . life and death." Catherine Leroy, "This Is That War," *Look*, vol. 32, no. 10, May 14, 1968, 24.

261   "I lose men . . . so many men." Ibid., 26–27.

262   "That people and nations . . . word *America*." William B. Arthur, Robert Meskill, Patricia Carbine, et al, "An Editorial," *Look*, vol. 32, no. 10, May 14, 1968, 33.

262   "We at *Look* believe . . . honorably as possible." Ibid., 33.

262   "I was not exactly . . . smell of death." John Killerlane, "This Amazing Female War Photographer Will Change Your Perception of the Vietnam War," historycollection.com/amazing-female-war-photographer-will-change-perception-vietnam-war/, accessed April 18, 2020.

264   "Absolutely, I wanted to be there." Winn, "What can photos."

264   "It's the biggest high . . . experience anywhere else." Jay Defoore, "Famed Vietnam War Photographer Catherine Leroy Dies at 60," *Popular Photography*, December 19, 2008, popphoto.com/photos/2008/12/famed-vietnam-war-photographer-catherine-leroy-dies-60, accessed September 12, 2018.

Epilogue

266   "Catherine has a great . . . marvelous image." Carol Squiers, "Catherine Leroy," *American Photography*, December 1988, 40.

268   "We were never sure . . . It did." Catherine Leroy, ed., *Under Fire: Great Photographers and Writers in Vietnam* (New York, Random House: 2005), XVII.

270   "What I did was to give war a face." Carol Pogash, "Reflecting on Shooting Through Decades of Battle," *New York Times*, April 21, 2005, nytimes.com/2005/04/21/arts/design/reflecting-on-shooting-through-decades-of-battle.html, accessed December 7, 2019.

Selected Bibliography

Books

Caputo, Philip. *A Rumor of War: The Classic Vietnam Memoir*. New York: Picador Henry Holt and Company, 2017.

Howe, Peter. *Shooting Under Fire: The World of the War Photographer*. New York: Artisan, 2002.

Leroy, Catherine, ed. *Under Fire: Great Photographers and Writers in Vietnam*. New York: Random House, 2005.

Leroy, Catherine. *Vietnam Narrative*. Translated by Sotires Eleftheriou, PDF Dotation Catherine Leroy, Paris, France (received by the author December 13, 2019).

McManus, John C. *Grunts: Inside the American Infantry Combat Experience, World War II Through Iraq*. New York: Penguin Publishing Group, 2010.

Ward, Geoffrey C., and Ken Burns. *The Vietnam War: An Intimate History*. New York: Penguin Random House, 2017.

Articles

Arthur, William B., Patricia Carbine, Robert Meskill, et al. "An Editorial," *Look*, May 14, 1968.

Blumberg, Arnold. "The First Battle of Khe Sanh." *Vietnam* magazine, August 2016. Available at: historynet.com/first-battle-khe-sanh.htm.

Clifton, Tony. "Catherine Leroy: French photographer whose images charted the horror of war from Vietnam to Beirut." *The Guardian*, July 20, 2006: 6. Available at: theguardian.com/news/2006/jul/21/guardianobituaries.france.

Defoore, Jay. "Famed Vietnam War Photographer Catherine Leroy Dies at 60." *Popular Photography*, December 19, 2008. Available at: popphoto.com/photos/2008/12/famed-vietnam-war-photographer-catherine-leroy-dies-60/.

Elbies, Jeffrey. "They Were Soldiers Once." *Popular Photography*, December 17, 2008. Available at: popphoto.com/how-to/2008/12/they-were-soldiers-once/.

Frank, Benis M. "Oral History Transcript: Lieutenant General Victor H. Krulak, US Marine Corps (Retired)." Historical Division, Headquarters, US Marine Corps, Washington, DC, 1973. Available at: usmcu.edu/Portals/218/LtGen%20Victor%20H_%20Krulak.pdf.

Freudenheim, Susan A. "A window on the war." *Los Angeles Times*, December 8, 2002. Available at: latimes.com/archives/la-xpm-2002-dec-08-ca-freuden-heim8-story.html.

Gabriner, Alice, and Lily Rothman, eds. "'Who Is The Enemy Here?' The Vietnam War Pictures That Moved Them Most." Undated photo essay, *Time*. Accessed July 2, 2020 at time.com/vietnam-photos/.

Herman, Elizabeth. "In Her Own Words, Photographing the Vietnam War," *New York Times*, September 27, 2017. Available at: lens.blogs.nytimes.com/2017/09/27/in-her-own-words-photographing-the-vietnam-war/.

Howe, Peter. "The Death of a Fighter: Catherine Leroy, 1944–2006." *Digital Journalist*, August 2006. Available at: digitaljournalist.org/issue0608/the-death-of-a-fighter.html.

Jackson, Derrick Z. "The Westmoreland mind-set," *New York Times*, July 22, 2005. Available at: nytimes.com/2005/07/22/opinion/derrick-z-jackson-the-west-moreland-mindset.html.

Leroy, Catherine. "A Remarkable Day in Hué: The enemy lets me take his picture." *Life*, February 16, 1968.

___. Interview by Marcel Giuglaris. Available at: dotationcatherineleroy.org/en/interviews1/with-catherine-leroy/.

Leroy, Catherine. "This Is That War." *Look*, May 14, 1968.

Squiers, Carol. "Catherine Leroy." *American Photography*, December, 1988: 30–41.

Winn, Steve. "What can photos teach us about war? Have a look." *San Francisco Chronicle*, April, 19, 2005.

Winslow, Donald R. "Vietnam War Photojournalist Catherine Leroy, 60." *NPPA News Archive*, July 11, 2006. Available at: https://nppa.org/news/2168.

Film and Video

Arnett, Peter. *Witness to War: Pulitzer Prize Winning Reporter Peter Arnett Talks about His Years in Vietnam*. Posted October 1, 2017. Available at: youtube.com/watch?v=e3DJiSO9MhI.

Faas, Horst. *Horst Faas on Catherine Leroy*. Filmed March 1, 2011, Munich, Germany. Available at vimeo.com/104250338.

Freedom Forum. *Remembering Horst Faas*. Posted May 11, 2012. Available at: youtube.com/watch?v=MzPH3GI8ZnA.

Menasche, Jacques. *Christian Simonpiétri on Catherine Leroy*, Paris, France, March 16, 2012. Available at: vimeo.com/104023209.

___. *Don McCullin on Catherine Leroy,* Paris, France, March 17, 2012. Available at: vimeo.com/104013791.

___. *The Hill Fights, Khe Sanh, April–May 1967*, excerpt from *Cathy at War*. Available at: vimeo.com/201391788.

Further Information

Catherine Leroy Fund: dotationcatherineleroy.org/en/

Reporters Without Borders: rsf.org/en

The Best We Could Do: An Illustrated Memoir by Thi Bui

Inside Out and Back Again by Thanhha Lai

Courageous Women of the Vietnam War: Medics, Journalists, Survivors, and More by Kathryn J. Atwood

Reporting Under Fire: 16 Daring Women War Correspondents and Photojournalists by Kerrie Logan Hollihan

Eyes of the World: Robert Capa, Gerda Taro, and the Invention of Modern Photojournalism by Marc Aronson and Marina Budhos

Most Dangerous: Daniel Ellsberg and the Secret History of the Vietnam War by Steve Sheinkin

Boots on the Ground: America's War in Vietnam by Elizabeth Partridge

Vietnam: A History of the War by Russell Freedman

Vietnamerica: A Family's Journey by G. B. Tran

Catfish and Mandala: A Two-Wheeled Voyage Through the Landscape and Memory of Vietnam by Andrew X. Pham

Acknowledgments

Tout d'abord, j'offre ma plus sincère gratitude to Robert Pledge and Dominique Deschavanne, cofounders of Dotation Catherine Leroy (DCL). Merci beaucoup for allowing me access to all of Catherine's materials, for being so helpful and supportive throughout this project. You were so generous in answering my many, many questions, and some of them twice! Sincere thanks to those who shared their memories of Catherine with me: Robert Pledge, cofounder and editorial director of Contact Press Images; DCL cofounder Fred Ritchin, Dean Emeritus of the International Center of Photography School in New York and founder and director of Pixel Press; photojournalist David Burnett; photographer Jan Goossens; and documentary photographer Ken Light at the UC Berkeley Graduate School of Journalism. Much gratitude to Dịu-Hương Nguyễn, PhD, assistant professor of history at the University of California, Irvine, for generously sharing her time and expertise. Dr. Nguyễn's research has focused on the social history of Việt Nam, in particular the voices and experiences of ordinary people during the Vietnam War. Acknowledgment to Ron Milam, PhD, for his expertise and for reading the manuscript. Dr. Milam is a Vietnam veteran, Fulbright Scholar to Việt Nam, teaches history at Texas Tech

University, and is the executive director of the school's Institute for Peace and Conflict. Any errors in the book are mine.

My heartfelt thanks to my agent, Steve Fraser, and my amazing editor, Howard Reeves, and I'm so grateful for the talented work of Sara Sproull, designers Melissa Jane Barrett and Heather Kelly, managing editor Megan Carlson, and production manager Kathy Lovisolo, as well as the great folks in Marketing and Sales, and everyone else at Abrams for making such beautiful books! Thanks to the wonderful librarians: Mollie Coffee at the Spokane Public Library and all those anonymous to me who fulfill my many interlibrary loan requests! To those librarians and history teachers so supportive of my books, and, of course, to the readers who love them!

To Donna Flannigan, Nina R. McCoy, and John Reilly, much gratitude for being my last-minute Vietnam connection. Thanks to Jennifer and Eric Akins for help with French, Cheryl Doran for helping me cut the boring parts, to all my writer friends for their unending support, and especially my sisters, for cheering me on!

With pride and gratitude, I acknowledge my dad, Harold Eugene Cronk, Eighty-Second Airborne, for assisting me in understanding the details of jumping out of a plane. With unending love and gratitude to Mike, for being my first reader and for loving and supporting me every day.

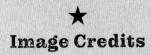

Image Credits

All photographs by Catherine Leroy or in the collection of and copyrighted by the Dotation Catherine Leroy except; 3 (top): National Museum of the US Air Force; 2 (bottom): Dudley Foster Collection, History of Aviation Collection, Special Collections and Archives Division, Eugene McDermott Library, University of Texas at Dallas; 8–9: United States Office of Strategic Services, Records of the Agency for International Development, National Archives; 12: United States Department of Defense, Department of the Army, Office of the Deputy Chief of Staff for Operations, National Archives; 14, 60 (top): Vietnam News Service; 17: US Air Force, National Archives; 18: US Army Signal Corps, National Archives; 20–21, 28–29: National Archives; 31, 51, 150, 160, 208, 253: Associated Press; 40: *Paris Match*; 44: US Marine Corps; 48–49: VA058597, US Army Aviation Museum Volunteer Archivists Collection, The Vietnam Center and Sam Johnson Vietnam Archive, Texas Tech University; 68–69: US Army; 88–89, 113: © Fondation Gilles Caron; 122: US Air Force; 131: VA058606, US Army Aviation Museum Volunteer Archivists Collection; The Vietnam Center and Sam Johnson Vietnam Archive, Texas Tech University; 136–137: US Information Agency; 174: Sgt J. S. Ryan/Marine Corps Photo; 186: Library of Congress; 211: US Navy; 267: Jan Goossens.

Index

Note: Page numbers in *italics* refer to illustrations.

anti-war demonstration, 185–87, *186*, 263

awards, 218, 249, 252, 253, *253*, 264, 268

Battalion Landing Team, 44, *44*

Battle of Huế, 236–45, *244*, 248

Battle of Ia Đrăng, 66–67

Bell, Van Daley, Jr., 94

Bird, Samuel, 70, 76, 80

Black Star, 123, 125, 140–41, 215, 218, 255

Bravo Company, 70–71, 73, 76–77

Browne, Malcolm W., 51, *51*

cameras, 61, 66, 203, 274, 276–77, *277*

Capa, Robert, 5

Caputo, Philip, 144

Catherine Leroy Fund, 273

children, 104–5, *104–5*

Collins, James Lawton, Jr., 125–26

colonialism, 6–7

combat jump, 126

compassion, 99, 111

Crandall, Bruce, 68–69, *68–69*

critics, 165

Crow's Foot, 85–86

Đà Nẵng, Vietnam, 45–46, 207, 219, 245

dangers, 167

Đặng Văn Phước, 112

Delta Company, 141

demilitarized zone (DMZ), 46, 85, 94

discouragement, 123

doctor, 100, *100*, 101

domino theory, 46–47

draft, 184

dreams, 272

Emerson, Gloria, 164

Emerson, Henry "Gunfighter," 56–57, 58–59

environmentalism, 269

F-100D, 2

Faas, Horst, 23, 27, 30, 32, 50–52, *51*, 183

film, 32–33, *275*, 275–76, *277*

first aid, 194–96, *196*

First Cavalry, 72, *72*, 78, *78*, 84, *84*

food, 90–91

Friedan, Betty, 41

Geneva Convention, 46
Golf Company, 175-76, 197-98
guerrilla family, 60, *60*
guerrilla soldiers, 142, *142*, 145, *145*, 147, *147*
guerrilla warfare, 57, 58
gunfire, 86-87

Harlem, New York, 255-56
helicopter, 59, 67, 68-69, *68-69*, 77
Hồ Chí Minh, 19, 20-21, *20-21*
Hồ Chí Minh Trail, 66
Huế, Vietnam, 223, 226, 236-45, *244*, 248

injuries, 60, *60*, 108, *108*, 110, *124*

jealousy, 161-62
Johnson, Lyndon B., 130, 135, 136-37, *136-37*
jumps, 126, 135, 151-55, *154*

Khe Sanh, Vietnam, 172-77, *174*, 179, *199*
Krulak, Victor, 101-2

Leica, 39, 61
Leroy, Catherine, 31, *31*, *64*, 113, *113*, *166*, 255
   adolescence, 38-39
   with award, 253, *253*
   in jump gear, 150, *150*

portrait, *267*
   with Sigholtz, 160, *160*
   on USS *Sanctuary*, 208
Leroy, Denise, 37, 38
Leroy, Jean, 38
letter, 270, *270*, 271
Life, 250-51, *250-51*
Look, 261-62

machine gun, 86-87
malaria, 130
marines, 108, *108*, *124*, 174, *174*, *199*, *241*
medical corpsman, 177, 179, *188-89*, 188-90
military advisers, 47, 48-49, *48-49*

napalm, 15, 17, *17*, 67, 176-77, 185
Ngô Đình Diệm, 47
Nixon, Richard, 263
North Vietnamese soldiers, 227-32, *265*

173rd Airborne Brigade, 88-89, *88-89*
Operation Junction City, 132, 134-35, 155-56
Operation Masher, 15-16, 86
Operation Rolling Thunder, 45-46
Operation White Wing, 16

pacification, 95, 98
Page, Tim, 112

paratroopers, 120, 122, *122*, 135, *155*

Paris Match, 4, 19, 22, 40, *40*

peasants, 95, 98, 103

poncho, 73, 76, 77

protests, 36-37, 185-87, *186*

punji pit, 14, *14*

radioman, 216-17, *216-17*

Ray, Michèle, 133-34

rebels, 12, *12*, 13

refugees, *224-25*, 224-26, 233, 237-39, *237-39*

rice paddies, 118, *118*, 119

rockets, 90

Rumpa, Raymond, 18, *18*

Sanctuary, USS, 203, 206-11, *208*, *211*

Screaming Eagles, 125

shrapnel, 202

Sigholtz, Robert H., 151, 160, *160*

Simonpiétri, Christian, 163

soldiers, 81, *81*, *183*, 228-29, *228-29*
   guerrilla, 142, *142*, 145, *145*, 147, *147*
   North Vietnamese, 227-32, *265*

soup, 102, 104-5, *104-5*

South Vietnamese Airborne Division, 122, *122*

souvenirs, 168

stringers, 50

tank, 28-29, *28-29*

Tân Sơn Nhất Airport, 3-4

temperatures, 26

terrain, 71, 119-20

Tết Offensive, 222, 233

Time, 266

tunnels, 13, 99

UH-1D Iroquois, 59, 68-69, *68-69*

Việt Minh, 7, 8-9, *8-9*, 19

war crimes, 146

Westmoreland, William, 102, 131, *131*, 132, 144, 146

Wike, Vernon, *188-89*, 188-90

women, Vietnamese, 96-97, *96-97*, 118, *118*, 260, *260*